Gramm Time
6

Illustrated by Peter Standley

Longman

Maria Carling

Grammar Time

6

Contents

Present tenses

present simple, present continuous, stative verbs,
present perfect simple, present perfect continuous

Welcome to the first issue of this year's *Teen Link* magazine!

My name is Isabella Hicks and, as some of you **know**, I'm *Teen Link*'s new Editor. Although I**'ve been working** on the magazine for only a short time, I must say, I absolutely **love** it!

This year we **are celebrating** four wonderful years of *Teen Link*. So, we**'ve been working** really hard and **have prepared** lots of fantastic articles and features for you!

We **hope** you have a great year with *Teen Link*!

Isabella Hicks,
Editor

Hello everyone!

Grammar reference

A	Form	

Tense	Affirmative, question, negative
Present simple	The postman always **comes** at eleven. **Does** the postman always **come** at eleven? The postman **doesn't** always **come** at eleven.
Present continuous	They **are sleeping** at the moment. **Are** they **sleeping** at the moment? They **aren't sleeping** at the moment.
Present perfect simple	We **have known** them since last year. **Have** we **known** them since last year? We **haven't known** them since last year.
Present perfect continuous	She **has been studying** English for six months. **Has** she **been studying** English for six months? She **hasn't been studying** English for six months.

B Present simple and present continuous

Present simple	Present continuous
We use the present simple: ▶ to refer to something which happens often or for a habit that we have. **I usually do my homework immediately after school.**	We use the present continuous: ▶ to describe something that is happening now. **Be quiet! I'm doing my homework.**
▶ to refer to permanent states **They live in England.**	▶ to describe temporary states and actions. **She's staying with her grandparents this week.**
▶ to talk about general truths or natural laws. **Water boils at 100° Celsius.**	▶ to describe states that are changing or developing. **Prices are rising very fast these days.**
▶ when we refer to programmes (cinema, theatre, etc.) or timetables (for ships, trains, etc.) **The film starts at 8.00pm.** **Our plane leaves at half past six.**	▶ to describe something that we plan to do in the immediate future. **We're leaving for France tomorrow.**
▶ to describe a sports fact or to tell the story of a film or book. **Andy Wilson scores his first goal!** **Sean Jameson, who plays the part of the detective, dies in a car crash.**	▶ to describe actions that are repeated and are annoying. In this case, we usually use adverbs such as always, constantly etc. **You're always borrowing my things without asking!**
Time markers Some time markers which we often use with the present simple are: ▶ adverbs of frequency: always, at present, today, these days, this sometimes, occasionally, never, rarely, seldom etc. ▶ other time markers such as every day/week/month, on Mondays Tuesdays, at the weekend, once a week/year etc.	Time markers Some time markers that we often use with the present continuous are: now, at the moment, at present, today, these days, this month/week, etc.

C   **Stative verbs**

There are some verbs that do not usually form continuous tenses (continuous forms) because they describe states, not actions. Some of these verbs are:
▶ verbs of the senses: see, hear, smell, feel, taste, sound, look, seem, notice, appear.
▶ verbs of perception: know, understand, think, believe, remember, forget, expect, etc.
▶ verbs that express likes or dislikes: like, dislike, love, hate, prefer, etc.
▶ other verbs such as: be, belong, have, need, want, cost, mean, wish, hope, include, contain, weigh, etc.

Some of the above verbs may also be used with continuous tenses. In this case, they have a different meaning since they describe actions, not states. Let's compare the examples below.

Have you seen the film? (see = see)	**I'm seeing Lucy after school.** (see = meet)
Her skin feels soft. (feel = it has a (soft) texture)	**She's feeling his face to see if it's hot.** (feel = touch)
Sugar tastes sweet. (taste = tastes)	**She's tasting the sauce.** (taste = try)
These flowers smell nice. (smell = be fragrant)	**She's smelling the flowers.** (smell = smell)
I think he's right. (think = believe, consider)	**I'm thinking about my new job.** (think = think)
Jack has two brothers. (have = have)	**Jack is having a bath.** (have = have (a bath))
That picture looks nice. (look = appear)	**He's looking at the picture.** (look = look)
He appears to be very friendly. (appear = appear/give the impression)	**He is appearing as Hamlet for the first time.** (appear = make an appearance)
He's selfish. (be = be)	**He's being selfish.** (be = behave, in a specific situation)

When we talk about somebody's appearance or feelings in a specific situation, the verbs **look** and **feel** may be used with simple or continuous tenses without changing the meaning of the sentence.
You look / are looking great!
I feel / am feeling tired.

He's appearing as Hamlet for the first time.

Grammar practice

1 Form sentences using the *present simple*.

Tip

Adverbs of frequency usually go before the main verb.

He usually goes to bed early.

He doesn't usually go to bed early.

Does he usually go to bed early?

The rest of the time markers usually go at the end or at the beginning of the sentence.

She goes to bed early every day.

In the mornings we have some cereal for breakfast.

1 we / have / dinner at eight (always)
   We always have dinner at eight.

2 what / you / do / after school? (usually)
   ....

3 Martin / visit / his parents in Southampton (once a week)
   ....

4 he / wear / ties (never)
   ....

5 she / fight / with her brother? (often)
   ....

6 you / go / to the cinema? (how often)
   ....

7 David / watch / horror films (seldom)
   ....

8 I / not work (at weekends)
   ....

9 he / go / to work by bus? (sometimes)
   ....

10 Danny / finish / work at 5.30 (every day)
   ....

11 we / write / to each other (rarely)
   ....

12 palm trees / grow / in warm climates (usually)
   ....

13 I / have / basketball practice (on Saturday morning)
   ....

14 she / cook / such wonderful meals? (always)
   ....

15 we / put away / our things? (at the end of the day)
   ....

2 Complete with the *present simple* or *present continuous*.

1 We always ......*stay*...... (stay) at the President Hotel when we're in Portsmouth.

2 Hey! I .... (talk) to you! Why .... (you / not listen) to me?

3 I .... (not see) her very often.

4 Hurry up! Alex and Bob .... (wait) for us.

5 What's so funny? Why .... (you / laugh)?

6 She's a teacher, but she .... (not work) at the moment.

7 .... (kangaroos / live) in Africa?

8 You .... (always / lose) your car keys!

9 I .... (never / eat) meat.

10 The population of India .... (grow) very fast.

11 How often .... (you / go) to the dentist?

12 Let's go. The film .... (start) at nine.

13 Harold .... (talk) to his girlfriend on the phone for hours every day.

14 The cost of living .... (go) up all the time.

3 Circle the correct answer.

1 That man over there *looks /(is looking)*at us.

2 Those colours *look / are looking* lovely on you.

3 *Do you think / Are you thinking* he's telling the truth?

4 I haven't decided yet. I *still think / am still thinking* about it.

5 They *have / are having* a lesson at the moment.

6 We *have / are having* a house in the country.

7 This perfume *smells / is smelling* fantastic. Why don't you buy it?

8 I *am / am being* very busy right now.

9 Mum *feels / is feeling* his forehead because he may have a temperature.

10 What's the matter? You *sound / are sounding* upset.

4 Complete with the *present simple* or *present continuous*.

1 What's the matter? Why <u>are you looking</u> (you / look) at me?

2 I've met Alice. She .... (be) a wonderful person.

3 Mr and Mrs Richards .... (have) six children.

4 She .... (taste) the meat to see if it needs more salt.

5 He .... (hate) cartoons.

6 I .... (think) it's a great idea!

7 Mary can't come to the phone right now. She .... (have) a shower.

8 .... (you / remember) my brother Mick?

9 I .... (not believe) you. You're lying!

10 Be quiet! I .... (think)!

11 I don't know why he .... (be) so rude. He's usually very kind.

12 That cake .... (taste) delicious.

13 Maya .... (see) Louis after dinner tonight.

14 That bag .... (belong) to me.

5 Complete with the *present simple* or *present continuous*.

1 That man ....<u>weighs</u>........ (weigh) 150 kilos.

2 Bill often .... (talk) about politics.

3 You .... (be) very selfish at the moment. You must apologise.

4 We .... (think) of moving to Liverpool.

5 Don't throw that book away. I .... (need) it.

6 He can't hear you. He .... (listen) to his personal stereo.

7 I .... (have) lunch at the moment. Can I call you back later?

8 .... (you / notice) anything strange in this room?

9 Kate's in her room. She .... (look) at the photos from Nick's party.

10 What .... (you / want)?

11 These keys .... (belong) to Mr Williams.

12 You .... (speak) too fast. I can't understand what you're saying.

13 Listen to them! They .... (make) a terrible noise in there!

14 How much .... (the shirt / cost)?

15 Leave me alone, please. I .... (try) to concentrate.

6 Read and complete. Use the *present simple* or *present continuous*.

Good evening. This is Mary Rose reporting for SBA Channel.

Good evening. This is Mary Rose reporting for SBA Channel. I'm at the Music Festival in Paris and I (1) ...<u>am having</u>... (have) a wonderful time! The French (2) .... (call) this festival 'La Fête de la Musique'. It (3) .... (take) place in June every year and (4) .... (last) for a week. The events (5) .... (start) early in the morning and (6) .... (not finish) until late at night. People (7) .... (sing) and (8) .... (dance) in the streets round the clock all day long.

Some very famous artists (9) .... (take) part in the festival this year. At the moment, we (10) .... (stand) near the Eiffel Tower. We (11) .... (listen) to 'Les Notes Heureuses', a popular French pop group. As you can see, people of all ages (12) .... (enjoy) themselves here!

D **Present perfect simple**

We use the **present perfect simple**:
▶ for an action that happened in the past at an indeterminable time. We do not refer to when the action happened because we do not know or it does not concern us.
I've met Sarah. She's a nice girl.
▶ to describe an action that happened in the past but that influences or has a visible effect on the present.
Dad has washed the car. It's clean.
▶ to refer to an action that started in the past and is continuing in the present.
Mr Allan has been a teacher for twenty-five years.
▶ to refer to an action that happened during a period of time that has not ended yet.
I've read three books this month.
▶ to talk about experiences that we have or have not had in our life.
Have you ever met anyone famous?
She's never had an accident before.
This is the funniest story I've ever heard.
This is the first time I've seen a lion.
▶ to refer to an action which has just been completed. In this case, we usually use just.
We have just had lunch.

Time markers
Some time markers that we often use with the present perfect simple are:
• **for:** We've known them **for** years.
• **since:** We've known them **since** 1992.
• **already:** It's only four o'clock, but he's **already** left.
• **yet:** Have you finished **yet**? They haven't called us **yet**.
• **just:** She isn't here. She has **just** left the building.
• **ever:** Have you **ever** eaten frogs' legs before?
• **never:** I have **never** heard that singer.
• **always:** She has **always** wanted to visit Spain.
• **lately/recently:** We haven't seen them **lately**.
• **so far:** They haven't made any mistakes **so far**.
• **today/this morning:** I have had two cups of coffee **this morning**.
• **How long...?:** **How long** have you been here?

E **Have gone to – have been to**

We use **have been to** to refer to the fact that somebody went somewhere in the past but has now returned.

We use **have gone to** to refer to the fact that somebody has gone somewhere and is still there and has not returned.
Sarah has been to Japan. (She has returned.)
Sarah has gone to Japan. (She is still there.)

7 Form sentences using the *present perfect simple*.

Tip
Already and just go before the passive participle.
Yet goes at the end of the sentence.
For refers to the duration of an action.
Since refers to the point in time when an action started.

1 I / eat / four sandwiches (today)
I have eaten four sandwiches today.

2 Charles / be / a fan of the Rolling Stones (always)
....

3 they / leave (already)
....

4 you / visit / Peru? (ever)
....

5 we / not do / the shopping (yet)
....

6 I / finish / my homework (just)
....

7 she / ride / a horse (never)
....

8 you / tidy / your room? (yet)
....

9 we / have / this car (for years)
....

10 I / not see / Tim (since Monday)
....

11 they / live / in this town? (how long)
....

12 we / hear / the good news (just)
....

8 Rewrite the sentences using the word given.

1 I've never driven a car before. **time**
This is the ....first time I've driven.... a car.

2 This is the first time we've visited Australia. **never**
We .... before.

3 I've never read such a good book before. **best**
This is the .... read.

4 She is the prettiest girl I've ever seen. **never**
I .... such a pretty girl before.

5 He has never done anything so silly before. **time**
This is the first .... anything so silly.

6 This is the first time I've tasted Chinese food. **have**
I .... Chinese food before.

7 This is the most beautiful country they've ever visited. **never**
They .... such a beautiful country.

9 Complete with the correct form of *have gone* or *have been*.

1 Aurora is not here at the moment. She ....has gone.... to the bank.

2 I .... just .... to the shops. Would you like to see my new dress?

3 Jake .... out. He won't be long.

4 The Smiths are on holiday. They .... to Ireland.

5 We .... never .... to France.

6 She isn't at home. She .... to the park.

7 Tim is on a business trip. He .... to Kent.

8 I .... to lots of countries but Greece is my favourite.

9 Myra .... to the supermarket. She'll be back in half an hour.

10 .... you ever .... to Moscow?

F | **Present perfect continuous**

We use the present perfect continuous:
▶ for an action that started in the past and is being repeated or is continuing until the present time.
I've been learning English for six years.
▶ for an action that has recently been completed. There is usually some indication in the present that this action has happened.
His clothes are dirty. He's been repairing the car.

Time markers
Some time markers that we often use with the present perfect continuous are: How long? for, since, recently, lately.

10 Read and complete. Use the *present perfect continuous*.

Mrs Elliott: Adam! You're covered in mud! What (1) ....have you been doing.... (you / do)?

Adam: I (2) .... (play) football.

Mrs Elliott: I (3) .... (look) everywhere for you, young man! (4) .... (you / play) football all this time? It's eight o'clock!

Adam: Oh, no! I'm late! I'm meeting Laura at nine. We're going to a concert.

Mrs Elliott: Oh no, you aren't. You're going straight to bed. You (5) .... (not sleep) enough.

Adam: But Mum, ...

Mrs Elliott: Don't argue with me, Adam! You (6) .... (spend) too much time with your friends lately. And you (7) .... (not do) very well at school.

Adam: But, Mum, I (8) .... (wait) for this concert for weeks! Please.

Mrs Elliott: Well, all right. But you have to promise you'll work harder from now on.

Adam: I promise! Thanks, Mum!

11 Rewrite the sentences using the word given.

1 He started working here three months ago. **has**
He <u>has been working here for</u> three months.

2 Kate started playing the violin when she was five. **been**
Kate .... since she was five.

3 She began reading three hours ago. **for**
She .... three hours.

4 Rob started learning English in 1998. **been**
Rob .... 1998.

5 I started cleaning the garage two hours ago. **have**
I .... for two hours.

6 Stanley started writing that article at two. **since**
Stanley has .... two.

7 It started raining an hour ago and it's still raining. **for**
It .... an hour.

8 Dad started watching TV at seven. **been**
Dad .... seven.

9 He started looking for a new job five months ago. **has**
He .... for a new job for five months.

10 The children began playing football at ten. **since**
The children .... ten.

11 The baby fell asleep an hour ago and she hasn't woken up yet. **sleeping**
The baby .... an hour.

12 We began digging in the garden this morning. **have**
We .... in the garden since this morning.

13 The police began looking for the missing child a few hours ago. **been**
The police .... for the missing child for a few hours.

14 They started eating at eight. **since**
They .... eight.

G Present perfect simple and present perfect continuous

Present perfect simple	Present perfect continuous
▶ With the **present perfect simple**, we refer to an action that has been completed. What interests us most is the result of this action. **She has washed the car. It's clean now.**	▶ With the **present perfect continuous**, the action may or may not have been completed. What interests us most is the action itself, not whether it has been completed. **She has been washing the car.**
▶ With the **present perfect simple**, we are not interested in the duration of the action but in the fact that it has been completed. **She has typed six letters today.**	▶ With the **present perfect continuous**, we emphasise the duration of the action that is continuing in the present. **She has been typing letters all morning and still has a lot to do.**

The verbs **work** and **live** are used in the same way in both the **present perfect simple** and the **present perfect continuous** without making any difference to the meaning of the sentence.
We have lived / have been living here since 1998.
He has worked / has been working at the office for six years.

12 Complete with the *present perfect simple* or *present perfect continuous*.

1   I _haven't played_ (not play) volleyball for a long time.

2   The children are very tired. They .... (play) volleyball.

3   She's a very famous writer. She .... (write) eleven books so far.

4   She .... (write) this book for a year. She hasn't finished it yet.

5   They .... (not be) to the theatre for ages.

6   You look really tired. What .... (you / do)?

7   I started reading this book a week ago. I .... (read) fifty pages so far.

8   I .... (not ride) a bike since I was nine.

9   He's got a very big stamp collection. He .... (collect) stamps since he was six.

10 .... (you / ever / travel) to another country?

11 Laura's in the attic. She .... (clean) it all day.

12 Sorry I'm late. .... (you / wait) long?

13 Sam .... (just / call) to say he'll be home late tonight.

14 I .... (not do) all my homework yet.

13 Complete with the *present simple, present continuous, present perfect simple* or *present perfect continuous*.

1   We always ...._visit_.... (visit) our grandparents on Sundays.

2   George is in his room. He .... (study) for his History test all day.

3   I .... (not talk) to you. I'm talking to Anne.

4   .... (you / ever / taste) Mexican food?

5   Please be quiet! You .... (always / complain) about something.

6   I'm tired. I .... (not sleep) enough lately.

7   How often .... (you / have) English lessons?

8   We can't buy the tickets. We .... (already / spend) all our money.

9   I .... (not watch) that film. You can switch the television off.

10 You're very quiet. What .... (you / think) about?

11 I .... (think) Paul is a wonderful person.

12 I .... (never / be) to Scotland.

13 The cake .... (taste) great. Can I have another piece?

14 Tina .... (just / come) back from work.

15 We .... (wait) here for half an hour and he hasn't come yet.

14 Rewrite the sentences using the word given.

1   Jack started working ten hours ago and he's still at work. **been**
    Jack ....._has been working for_..... ten hours.

2   She has never used a computer before. **time**
    It's the first .... a computer.

3   It started snowing on Tuesday and it hasn't stopped yet. **since**
    It .... Tuesday.

4   It's three weeks since I last spoke to Sarah. **not**
    I .... for three weeks.

5   He started talking ten minutes ago. **been**
    He .... ten minutes.

6   I last saw Mike in October. **have**
    I .... October.

7   They began looking for a house in May. **been**
    They .... a house since May.

8   I've never heard such a strange story. **ever**
    This is the strangest story .... heard.

9   She started typing that report two hours ago. **been**
    She has .... two hours.

10 I last went to the cinema a month ago. **for**
    I haven't .... a month.

15 Read and circle the correct answer.

USE OF
FCE
ENGLISH

Dear Julia,

I'm sorry I (1) ___a___ for such a long time, but I (2) .... hard these last few weeks. We're all very busy at the office. I (3) .... work at eight every evening, so I really (4) .... time for anything else!

The good news is that I (5) .... to Spain next week. Henry (6) .... two tickets for Madrid. We're leaving on Friday. I (7) .... been to Spain, so I can't wait! We (8) .... back on the 15th June. Then on the 17th we're travelling to Scotland to see our parents. We (9) .... them once a year. We'll be in Scotland for two weeks, so we can meet when you're back from your trip to Paris. What (10) ....? Write soon and let me know.

Love,

Marianne

1 (a) haven't written   b don't write   c hasn't written   d 'm not writing
2 a working   b 'm working   c 've been working   d work
3 a finishing   b finish   c 've finished   d finishes
4 a not have   b don't have   c am not having   d haven't been having
5 a fly   b flying   c 'm flying   d 've been flying
6 a has been buying   b buys   c have bought   d has bought
7 a haven't got   b never   c haven't had   d 've never
8 a 're coming   b coming   c 've come   d comes
9 a visit always   b 're visiting always c always visit   d 're always visiting
10 a do you think   b are you thinking   c have you thought   d have you been thinking

Writing practice Now you can do the **writing activity** for **Unit 1** (Teacher's Resource File).

Past tenses

past simple, past continuous, 'used to', 'would', past perfect simple, past perfect continuous

The 'No Parking' sign **wasn't** here ten minutes ago! Someone **put** it here after I **had parked** my car!

Grammar reference

A | **Form**

	Affirmative, question, negative	Time markers
Past simple	He **wrote** the letter on Monday. **Did** he **write** the letter on Monday? He **didn't write** the letter on Monday.	yesterday, three hours ago, last week, in 2001
Past continuous	She **was doing** her homework at 5.30. **Was** she **doing** her homework at 5.30? She **wasn't doing** her homework at 5.30.	while, as, all morning, at seven o'clock, yesterday
Past perfect simple	They **had gone** to bed by ten o'clock. **Had** they **gone** to bed by ten o'clock? They **hadn't gone** to bed by ten o'clock.	after, before, when, as soon as, until, already, just, by, by the time
Past perfect continuous	We **had been working** for hours. **Had** we **been working** for hours? We **hadn't been working** for hours.	since, for, all day
used to	I **used to go** to the cinema every Saturday. **Did** I **use to go** to the cinema every Saturday? I **didn't use to go** to the cinema every Saturday.	years ago, in the past, when I was young, always, often, sometimes, never
would	They **would sing** and **dance**. **Would** they **sing** and **dance**? They **wouldn't sing** and **dance**.	in the past, when I was young, always, usually, often, sometimes, never

B Past simple

We use the past simple:

▶ to describe an action that took place at a specific point in the past.
They left ten minutes ago.

▶ when we refer to habits or actions that happened often in the past.
He travelled a lot when he was younger.

▶ to refer to states that influence the past.
We lived in that house five years ago.

▶ to describe actions that happened consecutively, or one after another in the past.
She got up, had breakfast and went out.

C Past continuous

We use the past continuous:

▶ to describe an action that was developing at a specific time in the past.
I was doing my homework at eight o'clock yesterday evening.

▶ to refer to two or more actions that happened simultaneously in the past.
Mum was watching TV while dad was cooking dinner.

▶ to describe an action that was interrupted by another in the past.
We use the past continuous for the action that had the longest duration, and the past simple for the action of the shortest duration, the one that interrupted the first.
I was sleeping when the phone rang.
While she was drying the glasses, she dropped one.
As they were walking in the forest, they saw a deer.

▶ at the beginning of a story to describe the general atmosphere, the scene, before we start the narrative.
It was a beautiful morning. The sun was shining and the birds were singing.

Grammar practice

I Complete with the *past simple* or *past continuous*.

Tip

When is usually followed by the past **simple**.
While and as are usually followed by the past continuous.

1 We ..were waiting.. (wait) for the bus when it ....started.... (start) to rain.

2 I .... (see) Laura as I ....
(walk) down the street.

3 She .... (not hear) the doorbell
because she .... (listen) to music.

4 Jim .... (fall) asleep while he
.... (do) his homework.

5 They .... (not work) when I
.... (leave) the office.

6 Mr O'Sullivan .... (fix) his car when
I .... (see) him.

7 What .... (you / talk) about when I
.... (come) in?

8 Sheila .... (break) her leg as she
.... (walk) down the stairs.

9 .... (you / sleep) when I ....
(call)?

10 The TV .... (be) on but he
.... (not watch) it.

2 Complete with the *past simple* or *past continuous*.

1 He ......*had*....... (have) a shower and ......*left*....... (leave) for work.

2 At 10.30 last night, Jim .... (work) and Maria .... (watch) TV.

3 I .... (get) ready for bed when the phone .... (ring).

4 I'm sorry, I .... (not listen). Can you repeat that?

5 .... (you / call) the police when you .... (hear) the burglars?

6 We .... (not drive) fast but the police .... (stop) us.

7 The film .... (start) at 8.00 and .... (finish) at 10.00.

8 While the teacher .... (talk), I .... (think) about my birthday party.

9 He .... (not answer) the phone because he .... (not hear) it.

10 .... (Bruce / wait) for you when you .... (arrive) at the station?

11 What .... (you / do) at nine yesterday morning?

12 Mum .... (cut) her finger while she .... (cook).

3 Join the sentences with *as, while* or *when*. Do not change the order of the sentences.

Tip

When we refer to two actions that happened simultaneously, we only use **while**, not **when** or **as**.

1 Dad was reading his newspaper. Mum was cooking dinner.
   Dad was reading his newspaper while Mum was cooking dinner.

2 The boys were playing football. We were sitting in the garden.
   ....

3 I was walking the dog. I ran into Michael.
   ....

4 The sun was shining. We were walking along the river.
   ....

5 Peter was reading a comic. The teacher walked into the classroom.
   ....

6 I was driving down West Street. I saw an accident.
   ....

7 She was cleaning the house. I was tidying the attic.
   ....

8 He called. We were having dinner.
   ....

D **Past simple and present perfect**

Past simple	Present perfect
We use the **past simple**: ▶ for an action that happened at a specific point in the past. We mention when the action happened. **The game finished at 8.30.**	We use the **present perfect**: ▶ for an action that happened at an indeterminable time in the past. We do not mention when the action happened because we do not know or it does not concern us. **The game has finished.**
▶ for an action that started and was completed in the past. **He lived here for two years.** (He does not live here any more.)	▶ for an action that started in the past and is continuing in the present. **He has lived here for two years.** (He still lives here.)
▶ for an action that happened in the past, during a period of time that has ended. **I drank three cups of coffee this morning.** (It is no longer morning.)	▶ for an action that happened in the past during a period of time that has not ended yet. **I have drunk three cups of coffee this morning.** (It is still morning.)
When we use the **past simple**, we exclusively refer to the past.	When we use the **present perfect**, the actions that we are describing are connected with the present.

4 Circle the correct answer.

1 Bob (was)/ has been here a minute ago.
2 They *bought / have bought* this house in 1998.
3 We *lived / have lived* here since 1998.
4 Liam *came / has come* back from Paris last night.
5 I *didn't do / haven't done* my homework yet, so I can't come with you.
6 I *already read / have already read* this book.
7 What time *did you finish / have you finished* work yesterday?
8 Brenda *went / has gone* to the Bahamas last year.

5 Complete with the *past simple* or *present perfect simple*.

Tip

Remember the **time markers** that are used with the **past simple** and the **present perfect**.
Past simple: yesterday, ago, last week, in 1492
Present perfect simple: just, yet, already, for, since, ever, never, so far, up to now

Have you seen my new CD?

1 <u>Have you seen</u> (you / see) my new CD?
2 We .... (have) a wonderful time in Scotland last year.
3 I .... (not see) Carol at the party last night.
4 I .... (not see) John since Friday.
5 .... (you / ever / be) to Australia?
6 When .... (Paul and Sue / get) married?
7 Pam is on holiday. She .... (go) to Rome.
8 We .... (go) to Paris last year.
9 It's 10.30 and Simon .... (not call) yet.
10 I love London! I .... (live) here all my life.

6 Read and complete. Use the *past simple* or *present perfect simple*.

Isabella,
— Leslie (1) ...*came*... (come) to see you this morning. She (2) .... (look) worried. She (3) .... (not finish) the report for TeenLink yet. She needs your help. Call her.

—Ian (4) .... (call) at 10.30. He (5) .... (not leave) a message.

—Please go to the supermarket and get some orange juice for your Dad. I (6) .... (not have) time to do the shopping before work.
I (7) .... (be) too busy.

—Don't forget to feed the cats. They (8) .... (not eat) anything all day!

—Your lunch is ready. I (9) .... (leave) it on the kitchen table. Don't wait for Dad. He (10) .... (go) to the dentist, so he might be late.

Mum

7 Rewrite the sentences using the word given.

1 I haven't seen her since Monday. **saw**
I last ...*saw her on*... Monday.

2 The last time I spoke to Albert was a month ago. **for**
I haven't .... a month.

3 We haven't had a holiday since 1999. **had**
The last time .... was in 1999.

4 It hasn't rained since June. **last**
The .... was in June.

5 The last time she played tennis was in 1992. **since**
She .... 1992.

6 Sandra hasn't written to us for two weeks. **last**
Sandra .... two weeks ago.

7 Hugo last visited us in the summer. **since**
Hugo .... the summer.

E   Used to

▶ We use **used to** to describe actions that we have got used to doing (**repeated past actions**) in the past or states that influenced the past but no longer have any influence.
I used to play tennis when I was at school. (repeated past action)
We used to live in London when I was young. (state)

▶ Usually, we can replace **used to** with the **past simple** without changing the meaning of the sentence.
I played tennis when I was at school.
We lived in London when I was young.

▶ But when we describe a specific action that happened at a specific point in the past, we only use the **past simple**, not **used to**.
I got up late yesterday.
~~**I used to get up late yesterday.**~~ ✗

F   Would

▶ We can use **would** in the same way as **used to** to describe actions that we got used to doing in the past (**repeated past actions**).
When we were young, my sister and I would fight all the time.

▶ But when we describe states, not actions that influenced the past, we only use **used to**, not **would**.
Mr Wilson used to be a teacher.
~~**Mr Wilson would be a teacher.**~~ ✗

8 Complete with *used to* or the *past simple*. Use *used to* whenever possible.

1 I *used to go* (go) to work by bus but I bought a car last month.

2 I .... (not go) to work on Friday because I was ill.

3 .... (you / study) hard when you were a student?

4 What time .... (you / leave) the office yesterday?

5 I .... (play) the piano when I was your age.

6 We .... (not enjoy) the party last Saturday.

7 I .... (not like) spinach but now I love it!

8 He .... (be) very tired, so he went to bed early.

9 When you were a child, ... (you / go) to parties very often?

10 Hannah .... (go) to four parties last month.

11 Marvin .... (collect) toy soldiers but when he grew up, he lost interest in them.

12 The students .... (not enjoy) the excursion to the seaside because of the bad weather.

13 Why .... (she / be) angry with them yesterday?

14 There .... (be) a small cottage here but they pulled it down a few years ago.

9 Complete with *would* and the verb given.

When I was a child, we (1) *would visit* (visit) my grandparents on Sundays. They had a cottage by the sea.

Every morning, I (2) .... (always / go) fishing with my grandfather. My sister (3) .... (sometimes / come) with us. She (4) .... (simply / sit) and watch us. But she (5) .... (not let) us take any fish back home. Whenever we caught one, she (6) .... (take) it off the hook and throw it back into the water!

I (7) .... (get) really angry whenever she did that but Grandad (8) .... (laugh) about it. He didn't really mind. He thought it was sweet.

10 Write R for *repeated past action* or S for *state*. Then complete with *would* for repeated past actions and *used to* for states.

Tip

When we refer to states, not to repeated actions, we only use **used to**, not **would**.

1 When I was little, my mother ......would...... read to me every night. ......R......

2 That building ...used to... be a school. ...S...

3 On my birthday, I .... have a party and invite all my friends. ....

4 When I was younger, I .... go fishing every Saturday. ....

5 Years ago, she .... have long hair. ....

6 We .... have a house in Manchester years ago. ....

7 Grandma .... get up early and watch the sun rise every morning. ....

8 I .... like rock music but now I don't. ....

9 David .... live in that house. ....

10 When we were little, Dad .... always take us to the park on Sundays. ....

11 They .... have a house in the country but they sold it years ago. ....

12 When I was a teenager, I .... always go out on Saturdays. ....

13 He .... be an excellent swimmer when he was younger. ....

14 My aunt .... visit us every Sunday when she was still in London. ....

G | Past perfect simple and past perfect continuous

Past perfect simple	Past perfect continuous
We use the **past perfect simple**: ▶ to describe an action that happened in the past prior to another action. We use the **past simple** for the one that happened second. **By the time I arrived, Jack had already gone to bed.**	We use the **past perfect continuous**: ▶ to give emphasis to the duration of an action that happened prior to another action in the past. **I found my keys yesterday. I had been looking for them for days.**
▶ to describe an action that happened prior to a specific point in time in the past. **It was one o'clock in the morning. The guests had gone home.**	▶ to describe an action that happened in the past, that was of a long duration and when the result of it was visible in the past. **Her eyes were red. She had been crying.**
Time markers Some time markers that we often use with the **past perfect simple** are: **when, after, before, as soon as, until, just, already, by, by the time**, etc.	Time markers Some time markers that we often use with the **past perfect continuous** are: **since, for before, until**, etc.

H **Past time clauses**
We use the **past perfect simple** for an action that has already been completed prior to another action that happened in the past. We use the **past simple** for the second action.

But when we refer to two successive actions, ie. when the second action took place immediately after the first, then we can use the **past simple** for both of them.
The meaning is still the same.
I had locked the door before I left the house.
I locked the door before I left the house.

11 Complete with the *past simple* or *past perfect simple*.

1   By the time we .... *arrived* .... (arrive) at the cinema, the film *had already begun* (already / begin).

2   They .... (already / sell) that blue dress when I .... (get) to the shop.

3   Richard .... (just / finish) breakfast when I .... (wake) up.

4   As soon as the play .... (finish), we .... (leave) the theatre.

5   I .... (start) typing those letters before the boss .... (come).

6   I .... (not feel) so hungry after I .... (eat) that sandwich.

7   I only realised that I .... (meet) her a few years ago when I .... (see) her.

8   The bank .... (already / close) when I .... (leave) the office.

9   The meeting .... (start) by ten.

10 He .... (not find) my story interesting because he .... (hear) it before.

12 Rewrite the sentences.

1   She had never flown in a plane before.
    It was the first time *she had ever flown in a plane.*

2   I had never eaten Mexican food before.
    It was the first time ....

3   It was the first time Ned had ever driven a car.
    Ned ....

4   Mary had never made a chocolate cake before.
    It was the first time ....

5   It was the first time I had ever played golf.
    I ....

6   They had never used a monolingual dictionary before.
    It was the first time ....

7   It was the first time we had ever seen an eagle.
    We ....

13 Rewrite the sentences using the word given.

1   Magnus went home and Vera came later. **after**
    Vera *came after Magnus had gone* home.

2   First she locked the door and then she left for work. **before**
    She .... she left for work.

3   It was the first time I had ever seen such a boring film. **never**
    I .... such a boring film before.

4   She ate too much, so she had a stomach ache. **because**
    She had a stomach ache .... too much.

5   She went out and then I called her. **already**
    She .... when I called her.

6   We finished our lunch and then we left the restaurant. **soon**
    As .... our lunch, we left the restaurant.

7   I had never ridden a horse before. **ever**
    It was the first time .... a horse.

8   First he graduated from university and then he got a job. **after**
    He got a job .... from university.

14 Read and complete. Use the *past simple* or *past perfect simple*.

The Intruder

By Dudley Vince

When I came home from school that day, I (1) <u>realised</u> (realise) that I (2) .... (leave) my keys in my desk. I was about to go back and get them when I (3) .... (see) that the kitchen window was open. Dad (4) .... (forget) to close it that morning.

I climbed through the window and then I saw that the kitchen was a mess. Someone (5) .... (break) into our house! There was mud on the floor. The burglar (6) .... (break) my favourite cup and he (7) .... (even / eat) the chocolate biscuits that Mum (8) .... (leave) on the kitchen table for me!

I was terrified! I (9) .... (go) into the living room to call the police and realised that the 'burglar' (10) .... (not leave) the house. He was still in our living room, sitting on the sofa. The burglar was a big, fat cat! I must say, he was the friendliest burglar I had ever seen!

15 Form sentences using the *past perfect continuous*.

1 Anne was out of breath. (she / run)
<u>She had been running.</u>

2 People were sitting around the table with empty plates in front of them. (they / eat)
....

3 Her clothes were dirty. (what / she / do?)
....

4 Brian was exhausted. (he / travel / for eighteen hours)
....

5 There was a strong smell of garlic in the kitchen. (he / cooking)
....

6 I went to see the doctor on Friday. (I / not feel / well / for weeks)
....

7 Larry was very tired yesterday. (he / work / hard / all day)
....

8 The ground was wet. (it / rain / all night)
....

9 We were red and sore. (we / sunbathe / all morning)
....

10 They found the treasure at last. (how long / they / look for / it?)
....

16 Complete with the *past perfect simple* or *past perfect continuous*.

> **Tip**
> With the **past perfect continuous**, we give emphasis to the duration of the action.

1 We couldn't get in because we ...<u>had lost</u>... (lose) our keys.

2 She .... (sleep) for four hours when a loud noise woke her up.

3 Ray was terrified. He .... (never / be) in a plane before.

4 .... (it / stop) raining when you left the house?

5 We needed a rest. We .... (walk) all day.

6 By the time we got to the theatre, the play .... (already / begin).

7 I .... (wait) all evening before he finally came.

8 She didn't come with us because she .... (not finish) her homework.

9 How long .... (she / study) before she went to bed?

10 I was very tired. I .... (clean) the house all morning.

2

17 Read and complete. Use the *past simple, past continuous, past perfect simple* or *past perfect continuous*.

Boy's Adventure in Ridley Forest

Bobby Wilson, reunited with his parents, Martha and Charles.

Yesterday evening, Charles and Martha Wilson were finally reunited with their son, Bobby. By the time the police (1) _found_ (find) five-year-old Bobby, he (2) .... (wander) around Ridley Forest for four hours.

The Wilsons (3) .... (have) a picnic when Bobby (4) .... (decide) to explore the forest nearby. 'By the time we (5) .... (realise) that he

Ridley Forest

(6) .... (not be) with us, he (7) .... (already / walk) a very long distance,' said Mr Wilson.

When the police finally found Bobby, he (8) .... (lie) under a tree and he (9) .... (sleep).

'Well, I (10) .... (be) tired,' said young Bobby. 'I (11) .... (wait) for Mum to come and get me when I (12) .... (fall) asleep.'

18 Read the sentences. Some of them are correct and some have a word which should not be there. If a sentence is correct, put a tick next to it. If a sentence has a word which should not be there, write the word at the end of the line.

1	Mr Williams used to be a science teacher.	✓
2	She couldn't play because she had ~~been~~ broken her leg.	*been*
3	Oliver was tired because he had been writing letters all morning.	....
4	We did arrived at the station at 7.30.	....
5	Georgia has left ten minutes ago.	....
6	I saw Jane while I was walking home from work.	....
7	We weren't being at home at ten o'clock last night.	....
8	He would always to bring flowers when he came to visit.	....
9	Had they been finished their homework?	....
10	The Smiths used lived in that house ten years ago.	....

19 Read and circle the correct answer.

This (1) ..ª.. to me three years ago. It was my fifteenth birthday and I was having a party. I (2) ..... for that day for weeks! I had invited all my friends, even people I (3) ..... for a very long time. I (4) ..... everything by six o'clock. My friends started coming at seven.

Everyone (5) ..... by half past seven and it was time to bring out my birthday cake. My guests all stood around the table and I went into the kitchen to get the cake. As I (6) ..... it, I (7) ..... over my little brother's toy train and fell. The cake landed on my face and I (8) ..... on the floor, covered in cream and strawberries! My friends thought it was funny. They (9) ..... all night.
I (10) ..... so embarrassed in my life!

1 ⓐ happened	b has happened	c was happening	d had happened
2 a have waited	b had been waiting	c was waiting	d waited
3 a didn't see	b haven't seen	c wasn't seeing	d hadn't seen
4 a prepared	b have prepared	c had prepared	d had been preparing
5 a was arriving	b had been arriving	c had arrived	d would arrive
6 a carried	b was carrying	c had carried	d had been carrying
7 a tripped	b was tripping	c have tripped	d had tripped
8 a have lain	b had lain	c lay	d used to lie
9 a have laughed	b would laugh	c laughed	c used to laugh
10 a never felt	b have never felt	c was never feeling	d had never been feeling

20 Read and complete. Use the *past simple*, *past continuous*, *past perfect simple* or *past perfect continuous*.

❖ • ❖ Out of luck ❖ • ❖ • ❖

Tom (1) .....was..... (be) on his way to visit his parents. He (2) .... (drive) for twenty minutes when his car (3) .... (break down). He (4) .... (get) out of the car and (5) .... (try) to find out what the problem was. No luck! He (6) .... (not know) much about cars. All he (7) .... (know) was that his car (8) .... (break down) in the middle of nowhere and that he (9) .... (stand) in the rain, hoping that someone would help him.

He (10) .... (wait) for more than an hour when a lorry driver (11) .... (offer) to drive him to his parents' house. They (12) .... (get) there in twenty minutes. Tom (13) .... (thank) the driver, got out of the car and (14) .... (ring) his parents' doorbell. There (15) .... (be) no answer. He rang again. No one (16) .... (open) the door. He couldn't believe how unlucky he was! His parents (17) .... (go) out and there he was again, standing in the rain, waiting for someone to drive him back home. 'This surprise visit wasn't such a good idea after all,' he thought to himself.

Writing practice Now you can do the **writing activity** for **Unit 2** (Teacher's Resource File).

The Future

'will', 'going to', present continuous, present simple,
future continuous, future perfect simple,
future perfect continuous

Grammar reference

A	Form			
		Affirmative	Question	Negative
	will	I will write the letters.	Will I write the letters?	I won't write the letters.
	going to	You are going to write the letters.	Are you going to write the letters?	You aren't going to write the letters.
	Future continuous	He will be writing the letters.	Will he be writing the letters?	He won't be writing the letters.
	Future perfect simple	She will have written the letters.	Will she have written the letters?	She won't have written the letters.
	Future perfect continuous	They will have been writing the letters.	Will they have been writing the letters?	They won't have been writing the letters.

B Will

We use will:
- to make a prediction, to say what we believe will happen in the future. We usually use it with expressions such as **I think, I believe, I bet, I expect, I am sure/afraid, I suppose, I hope,** or adverbs such as probably, perhaps, possibly, certainly etc.
  I'm sure she'll pass the exam.
  I'll probably be at school early tomorrow morning.
- for decisions that we make spontaneously, at the time when we are speaking.
  The phone's ringing. I'll answer it.
- to offer our help to somebody.
  I'll help you with your homework.
- to make a promise.
  I promise I won't be late.
- to ask somebody to do something for us.
  Will you open the door for me?
- to warn somebody about something.
  Be careful! You'll hurt yourself with that knife.
- to talk about something that will definitely happen in the future because it is inevitable, we cannot change or control it using external factors.
  The sun will rise at 6.35 tomorrow.
  The temperature will drop during the weekend.

C Going to

We use going to:
- when we refer to future plans, to something that we intend to do in the future.
  We're going to buy a new car next month.
- when we know that something is going to happen in the future because there is something in the present that shows us this, an indication.
  Look at those clouds. It's going to rain.

D Present continuous

We use the present continuous to refer to something that we have already planned to do in the immediate future. We are sure that the action that we are talking about will happen.
We're flying to London tomorrow.

E Present simple

We can use the present simple for the future, when we refer to programmes (cinema, theatre, etc.) or timetables (for ships, trains, etc.).
Our bus leaves at 6.30.
The play finishes at eleven o'clock.

3

Grammar practice

1 Complete with *will* or *going to*.

1 Don't worry. I ....'ll show.... (show) you how the camera works.

2 Don't wait up for me. I .... (probably / be) home late tonight.

3 Jordan has sold his car because he .... (buy) a new one next month.

4 According to the weather forecast, there .... (be) heavy rain in the south on Wednesday.

5 I've bought a new dress and I .... (wear) it to the party tonight.

6 What .... (you / do) this weekend? Have you decided?

7 I promise I .... (not tell) anyone about this.

8 Autumn is almost over. It .... (get) colder soon.

9 I've been thinking about this for weeks. I .... (not accept) that new job.

10 It's really hot in here. .... (you / open) the window, please?

2 Circle the correct answer.

1 A: Did you remember to book a table?
  B: Oh, no! I forgot. I (will)/ am going to call the restaurant now.

2 A: Why do you need Craig's phone number?
  B: I 'll / 'm going to invite him to my party.

3 A: I'm going out with Alice tonight.
  B: Oh, really? Then I 'll / 'm going to come with you.

4 A: Mike called this morning.
  B: Yes, Mum told me. I will / am going to call him later.

5 A: So, what are your plans for the summer?
  B: I will / am going to visit my cousin in Scotland.

6 A: Jill has passed her exam.
  B: Really? That's great! I will / am going to call her and congratulate her.

7 A: Would you like something to eat?
  B: Yes, thank you. I will / am going to have a sandwich.

8 A: Do you really need all those eggs?
  B: Yes, I do. I will / am going to make an omelette.

3 Complete with *will* or *going to*.

Tip

Will is for making general predictions, to say what we believe will happen in the future. **Going to** is for making predictions when we are sure that something will happen in the future because there is an indication of it in the present.

1 I'm sure you ....'ll have...... (have) a great time at the party.

2 Look at those cars. They .... (crash)!

3 I expect they .... (be) on time.

4 We .... (be) late! The film starts in ten minutes and Ben is still in the shower!

5 I feel dizzy. I .... (faint).

6 You should talk to Jane. I'm sure she .... (understand).

7 Look out! That branch is broken! It .... (fall)!

8 Do you think the team .... (win) the match on Saturday?

9 The oven is too hot. The cake .... (get) burnt.

10 The boat is leaking badly. It .... (sink).

4 Complete with *will* or the *present continuous*.

1 – Would you like something to drink?
  – Yes, please. I .....'ll have..... (have) an orange juice.

2 I can't come with you on Sunday. I .... (have) dinner with Tina.

3 You look tired. I .... (make) you a cup of tea.

4 Bob .... (come) to see us tonight.

5 .... (you / post) this letter for me?

6 .... (you / do) anything tomorrow morning?

7 Oh no! I forgot to call Violet. I .... (call) her now.

8 We .... (fly) to Madrid on Friday. Here are our tickets.

9 I .... (meet) James for lunch at 12.30.

10 I'm really tired. I think I .... (go) straight to bed.

5 Read and complete. Use the *present continuous* or *present simple*.

□ | ⊑ untitled | 回目

✉

From: Amanda Clarke

To: Caroline Beecham

Subject: Our meeting

Dear Caroline,

I'm afraid we can't meet you tomorrow.

The weekly meeting (1) _finishes_ (finish) at 17.00 and I have to be at the airport at 17.30.

You see, my mother (2) .... (come) to visit. Her plane (3) .... (arrive) in London at 17.30 and I (4) .... (pick) her up from the airport.

Then, in the evening I (5) .... (take) her to the theatre. The play (6) .... (begin) at 20.00 and it (7) .... (not finish) until 22.30.

But I (8) .... (not work) this Monday, so we can meet then if you're not busy. What do you say?

Love,

Amanda

PS The art exhibition (9) .... (open) next week. Do you want to go?

> **Tip**
>
> Remember:
> The **present continuous** is for referring to something that we have already planned to do in the future.
> The **present simple** is for referring to programmes (theatre, cinema) or timetables (for trains, aeroplanes, etc.)

F **Future continuous**

We use the **future continuous**:
▶ to refer to an action that will develop at a specific point in the future.
  At 9.30 tomorrow morning, we'll be travelling to Manchester.
▶ to ask somebody about his future plans, particularly when we want him to do something for us.
  – **Will you be passing the library on your way home?**
  – **Yes. Why?**
  – **Could you return this book for me?**
▶ to refer to an action that will definitely take place in the future, either because it forms part of a plan or because it is a routine action.
  I'll be seeing him tomorrow. We always meet on Mondays.

6 Complete with the *future continuous*.

1 I'll be at home at 8.30 tonight. I _'ll be watching_ (watch) the football match.

2 .... (they / work) all day tomorrow?

3 Don't call him before nine. He .... (sleep).

4 What .... (you / do) this time next week?

5 I .... (not use) my car tonight. You can borrow it.

6 Sue .... (have) lunch with Alan at 1.30 tomorrow.

7 .... (you / pass) the chemist's on your way home? I need some aspirin.

8 They .... (not stay) with us. They've booked a room at the Palace Hotel.

9 This time next week we .... (lie) on the beach.

10 I .... (see) Tom at the office tomorrow. I can give him your message.

7 Complete with *will* or the *future continuous*.

1 We're going to the park. We ..... won't be ..... (not be) long.

2 At one o'clock tomorrow, she .... (have) lunch with her new boss.

3 .... (you / see) Julia tomorrow? I have a message for her.

4 That suitcase looks heavy. I .... (carry) it for you.

5 Don't worry. I'm sure you .... (pass) the exam.

6 They .... (travel) all day tomorrow, so I'm sure they .... (be) tired when they arrive.

7 Come on. I .... (show) you my new computer.

8 I .... (drive) past the baker's on my way home. Do you want some bread?

9 She .... (practise) the piano tomorrow, as she always does.

10 This .... (not happen) again. I promise.

G Future perfect simple

We use the **future perfect simple** to refer to an action that will have already been completed before a specific point in the future. **I will have finished this book by next week.**

Often, the **future perfect simple** is used with time markers such as: **by, by the time, before** etc.

H Future perfect continuous

We use the **future perfect continuous** to refer to an action that will continue until a specific point in the future. **She will have been working here for ten years in January.**

8 Read and complete. Use the *future perfect simple*.

Simon is twenty. He wants to be an actor. He (1) will have finished (finish) his studies by the end of this year and he hopes that he (2) .... (become) well known by the time he's twenty-five. What (3) .... (he / do) by the time he's forty-five?

By the time I'm thirty:
4 I .... (move) to the USA.
5 I .... (buy) a house in Hollywood.

By the time I'm thirty-five:
6 I .... (appear) in many films.
7 I .... (make) a lot of money.

By the time I'm forty-five:
8 I .... (win) many acting awards.
9 I .... (write) my autobiography.
10 I .... (direct) my first film.

9 Form sentences using the *future perfect continuous*.

1 Tom / watch / TV / for six hours by 7.30
Tom will have been watching TV for six hours by 7.30.

2 by December / he / work / here for a year

3 I / learn / English / for five months in March

4 how long / you / study / medicine / by the end of this year?

5 the boys / play / football / for three hours by five o'clock

6 Sue / drive / her new car / for three weeks on Friday

7 we / live / in London / for fifteen years in May

8 by the time he arrives / he / travel / for over twenty-four hours

> **I** **Future time clauses**
>
> Clauses that are introduced by time links are called **time clauses**.
> Some time links that may be referred to in the future are: **when, before, after, as soon as, until, by, by the time.**
> Even if they refer to the future, these links are followed by the **present simple**.
> **I'll give him your message when I see him.**
> ~~**I'll give him your message when I will see him.**~~ ✗
>
> Let's see another example.
> **By the time I get home, they will have gone to bed.**
> In the above clause, the **time clause** is followed by the **present simple**, and the main clause is in the **future perfect**.

10 Match the two parts of each sentence.

1	You'll feel much better after	a	the train will have left.
2	When Mum goes to the supermarket,	b	until I find that photo.
3	He'll tell us all about his trip to London	c	she'll get us some more popcorn.
4	I will have tidied my room	d	I have the money.
5	By the time we get to the station,	e	by the time Mum gets back.
6	I'll pay you back when	f	as she arrives.
7	I won't stop looking	g	when he comes back.
8	She will phone as soon	h	you get some rest.

11 Circle the correct answer.

1 We *call* / *will call* you when we *get* / *will get* back home.

2 Don't worry. We *clean* / *will clean* up that mess before Mum *sees* / *will see* it.

3 I *start* / *will start* working on that article as soon as I *get* / *will get* to the office.

4 Lunch *is* / *will be* ready when you *come* / *will come* home.

5 As soon as we *find* / *will find* a bigger house, we *move* / *will move*.

6 I *type* / *will type* these letters before the boss *comes* / *will come*.

7 When everyone *is* / *will be* here, we *bring* / *will bring* out the cake.

8 She *phones* / *will phone* as soon as she *sees* / *will see* our message.

9 Her dad *doesn't let* / *won't let* her leave the house until she *apologises* / *will apologise*.

10 I *am* / *will be* here when the guests *start* / *will start* arriving.

12 Complete with *will*, the *present simple*, *future continuous* or *future perfect simple*.

1 I ....'ll call.... (call) you as soon as I ......get...... (get) home.

2 Jane .... (finish) her homework before she .... (go) to bed tonight.

3 We .... (go) shopping as soon as it .... (stop) raining.

4 I .... (wait) for you when your bus .... (get) there.

5 By the time we .... (arrive) at the cinema, the film .... (start).

6 I .... (let) you know as soon as I .... (hear) from her.

7 Don't worry. I promise I .... (go) to the bank before it .... (close).

8 When I .... (see) him, I .... (give) him your message.

9 As soon as we .... (have) enough money, we .... (buy) a new car.

10 I .... (go) to bed by the time they .... (come) back.

J | **The Future: summary**

Form	Use	Example
will	▶ prediction	I'm sure you'll **enjoy** the film.
	▶ instantaneous or spontaneous decision, promise, request, warning	They're here. **I'll open** the door. **I'll help** you with your homework.
	▶ certain (inevitable) action in the future	There **will be** a solar eclipse at 4.20 tomorrow.
going to	▶ future plan, intention	They're **going to get** married.
	▶ prediction (which there is an indication of in the present)	Look at those clouds. It's **going to rain.**
Present continuous	▶ planned personal action for the immediate future	He's **leaving** for Spain tomorrow.
Present simple	▶ programmes (theatre, cinema, etc.), timetables (for buses, trains, etc.)	The film **starts** at six.
Future continuous	▶ action developing at a specific point in the future	We'll **be having** dinner at 7.30 tonight.
	▶ certain action in the future (part of a plan or routine)	**I'll be working** all day on Monday.
	▶ to ask about somebody's future plans	**Will** you **be using** your computer this evening?
Future perfect simple	▶ action that will be completed by some point in the future	We **will have arrived** by three o'clock.
Future perfect continuous	▶ action that will continue until some point in the future	We **will have been living** here for three years in May.

13 Complete with the correct form of the verb.

1   A: We haven't got any milk.
    B: It's OK. I ......'ll go...... (go) and get some.

2   A: So, you're leaving tomorrow.
    B: Yes, I am! This time next week, I
    .... (swim) in Hawaii!

3   A: Is 6.30 all right?
    B: No, sorry. At 6.30 tomorrow evening, I
    .... (study) for an English test.

4   A: How long have you been working here?
    B: By the end of this month, I ....
    (work) in this office for ten years.

5   A: Where are you going?
    B: Out. I .... (not be) long, I
    promise.

6   A: What time .... (your plane / leave) tomorrow?
    B: At half past eight.

7   A: Why have you moved all the furniture out of your room?
    B: I .... (paint) it tomorrow.

8   A: Will you still be at work at 5.30?
    B: Yes. I .... (not finish) my report by then.

9   A: Please tell Jim about the party next Saturday.
    B: Of course. I'll tell him as soon as I
    .... (see) him.

10 A: Would you like to come with us tomorrow?
    B: I'm sorry. I can't. I .... (meet) Georgia tomorrow afternoon.

14 Read and circle the correct answer.

Teen Link

Robo News

by Danny MacKee

Ninety per cent of all robots today are used in factories. Soon (1) *there will have been* / *there will be* robots that can do almost anything. Here are some 'robofacts' that you (2) *will definitely find* / *will definitely be finding* very interesting.

RoboDoctors: Today robots are used in hospitals to help doctors with some very simple tasks. Some experts predict that by the end of the 22nd century, robots (3) *will have been replacing* / *will have replaced* doctors. They (4) *are performing* / *will perform* even the most difficult operations without the help of humans.

RoboNauts: Scientists have already sent robots to Mars. Soon they (5) *will be sending* / *will have been sending* them to other planets as well. The robots which are used to explore space today are controlled by astronauts. In the next few years, scientists (6) *will have designed* / *will have been designing* robots that can travel into space alone.

RoboDrivers: Robots have been working in car factories for many years. In the future, they (7) *will be driving* / *will have been driving* cars too! Scientists are already working on the first robot-controlled taxis, so some robots (8) *will have worked* / *will be working* as taxi drivers!

Experts predict that the number of robot manufacturers (9) *will have doubled* / *double* by the end of this century. Robots (10) *will be becoming* / *will become* part of everyday life and they (11) *will definitely make* / *will definitely have been making* it easier. Don't you just love technology?

Oral practice Now you can do the **oral activity** for **Unit 3** (Teacher's Resource File).

Question tags, short agreements

Grammar reference

A Question tags

Form

▶ Question tags are formed by an auxiliary verb and the personal pronoun that corresponds to the subject of the clause. They always go at the end of the clause and are separated from this by a comma. The auxiliary verb that we use for the **question tag** depends on the tense that the clause is in.
He lives in that house, doesn't he?
You aren't talking to me, are you?

▶ When the clause is positive, we use a negative **question tag**.
When the clause is negative, we use a positive **question tag**.
He's coming with us, isn't he?
You didn't forget to call Mark, did you?

▶ When there is a **modal verb** in the clause, the **question tag** is formed by using this.
He can't hear very well, can he?

▶ The **question tag** for I am is **aren't I?**
I'm wrong, aren't I?
~~I'm wrong, amn't I?~~ ✗

▶ The **question tag** for let's is **shall we?**
Let's go home, shall we?

▶ When the clause is in the imperative, the **question tag** both in the positive and the negative is **will you?**
Be quiet, will you?
Don't shout, will you?

► The **question tag** for **have got** is formed using **have** or **has**. But when **have** is the main verb, the **question tag** is formed using the auxiliary verb **do/does/did**.
She's got a brother, hasn't she?
You always have cereal and coffee for breakfast, don't you?

► When we have **there is/are, there was/were, there will be** etc., the **question tag** in the clause, the **question tag** is formed using **there**, not **it** or **they**.
There's a cinema near your house, isn't there?
~~There's a cinema near your house, isn't it?~~ ✗
There were a lot of people at the beach, weren't there?
~~There were a lot of people at the beach, weren't they?~~ ✗

► When the subject of the clause are the words **this/that** or **these/those**, we use **it** or **they** in the **question tag**.
That's Mary's car, isn't it?
These are your sunglasses, aren't they?

► When the subject of the clause is a word such as **somebody, everyone, no one**, we use **they** and a plural verb in the **question tag**.
Everyone was at the party, weren't they?

► When the subject of the clause is a negative word such as **nothing, no one, nobody**, the **question tag** is positive.
No one saw us, did they?

Use
► We use **question tags** when we are not absolutely sure about something and we want to confirm it, to find out whether or not it applies.
You live in London, don't you?

► Often we use them when we are sure about something and are simply waiting for our fellow speaker to agree with us.
It's a lovely day, isn't it?

Grammar practice

1 Complete with a *question tag*.

1 Our train leaves at six, _doesn't it?_
2 Sue wasn't at the party last night, ...?
3 He's told you about the meeting, ...?
4 They're coming back tomorrow, ...?
5 You haven't been waiting long, ...?
6 You don't like him very much, ...?
7 They're going to move to Bristol, ...?
8 It had stopped raining when you went out, ...?
9 He didn't call, ...?
10 You weren't talking to me, ...?
11 She isn't your friend, ...?
12 You won't tell anyone you saw me, ...?
13 The cat doesn't sleep on your bed, ...?
14 They'll be arriving tomorrow, ...?

2 Complete with a *question tag*.

1 I should apologise, _shouldn't I?_
2 You've got a house in the country, ...?
3 Let's have something to eat, ...?
4 There's too much noise in here, ...?
5 You always have lunch at one, ...?
6 He can't drive, ...?
7 You've never lied to me, ...?
8 Someone told you about it, ...?
9 Don't play with that machine, ...?
10 No one helped you, ...?
11 I'm too late, ...?
12 Stop looking at me, ...?
13 That's Jim's wife over there, ...?
14 Ms Clark used to be a teacher, ...?
15 Everybody enjoyed the holiday, ...?

4

3 Complete with a *question tag*.

1　I look awful, _don't I_?
2　There are enough sandwiches for everyone, ...?
3　You won't tell anyone, ...?
4　Let's go out tonight, ...?
5　Bill has to make a speech, ...?
6　The film was excellent, ...?
7　I'm fat, ...?
8　You weren't sleeping when I called, ...?
9　Don't ask so many questions, ...?
10　You will have finished by three, ...?

4 What would you say in the following situations? Write sentences using a *question tag*.

1　You have arranged to meet your friend tonight but you're afraid he'll be late. What do you say?
You won't be late, will you?

2　You think your friend, Madge, is having a birthday party on Saturday but you're not sure. Ask another friend.
....

3　You think your friend has never eaten Thai food. Check.
....

4　You want to make sure that your friend will call you later. What do you say?
....

5　You think your friend bought a new bike last week. Check.
....

6　You're trying to do your homework but your sister is making too much noise. What do you say?
....

7　It's a very hot day. You phone your friend and suggest going to the beach.
....

8　You're talking to your friend but you don't think he's listening to you. What do you say?
....

9　You've found a pair of sunglasses and you think they're your friend's. Ask him.
....

10　You don't think your brother has done his homework yet. Check.
....

B　Short agreements

▶ We use **so** and **neither** or **nor** to agree with something that somebody is saying to us, without repeating what he said to us.
▶ To agree with a positive sentence, we use **so + auxiliary/ modal verb + subject.**
– I'm very tired.
– So am I.
▶ To agree with a negative sentence, we use **neither/nor + auxiliary/modal verb + subject.**
– Sam didn't pass the test.
– Neither did Alex.

5 Complete with the correct *auxiliary verb* or *modal verb*.

Tip

When the verb in the sentence with which we agree has a **modal verb**, we use the **modal verb** and in **short agreement** too.

1　A: I love pop music.
　　B: So _do_ I.

2　A: I didn't like the film.
　　B: Neither .... I.

3　A: Sarah used to have long hair.
　　B: So .... Mary.

4　A: I've never been to Italy.
　　B: Nor .... I.

5　A: Chris isn't coming with us.
　　B: Neither .... David.

6　A: I'd like some orange juice.
　　B: So .... I.

7　A: I don't work on Saturdays.
　　B: Nor .... I.

8　A: I could read when I was five.
　　B: So .... I.

9　A: We had a great time last night.
　　B: So .... we.

10　A: I can't remember her name.
　　B: Neither .... I.

11　A: I should really go to bed soon.
　　B: So .... I.

12　A: I've got a headache.
　　B: So .... I.

6 Reply with *so* or *neither/nor* using the word given.

1 Will is very interested in History. (George)
So is George.
....

2 Tina left early last night. (Anne)
....

3 I've never met anyone famous. (I)
....

4 We must leave soon. (we)
....

5 Brian failed the exam. (Kate)
....

6 I don't believe her. (I)
....

7 Charlotte has bought a new car. (Alex)
....

8 I can't answer this question. (I)
....

9 He'll never forgive them. (I)
....

10 I was born in 1989. (my brother)
....

7 Read and complete. Use only one word in each space.

USE OF FCE ENGLISH

Diane: Dad! You haven't been standing there long, (1) ....*have*.... you?

Dad: No, I haven't. Why?

Diane: Nothing. Just asking.

Dad: What's the matter? You look funny. You aren't ill, (2) .... you?

Diane: Er, no. I'm just tired, that's all.

Dad: So (3) .... I. And I haven't finished my work yet.

Diane: (4) .... have I.

Dad: OK, then. We both have a lot of things to do, don't (5) ....? Why don't you go to your room and let me finish my report?

Diane: What's the rush? There's plenty of time after dinner, isn't (6) ....? Now tell me about your business trip to Barcelona next week, (7) ....you? You've never been to Spain before, (8) .... you?

Dad: No, I haven't. Now, sweetheart, I'm busy. Let me get on with my work, (9) .... you?

Diane: But ...

Dad: What are you hiding behind your back? You've done something to my computer, (10) .... n't you? What's happened to my computer?

Diane: Er ... Let me explain ...

Dad: Diane!!

Oral practice Now you can do the **oral activity** for **Unit 4** (Teacher's Resource File).

Revision 1-4

1 Read and circle the correct answer.

Dear Marianne,

Thanks for your letter. It was great to hear from you.

So you (0) ..c.. some time off work! That's great – you (1) ..... it. You (2) ..... too hard lately.

Tom and I (3) ..... to Paris after all. We (4) ..... of moving to a bigger house in June. I (5) ..... this one very much and neither (6) ..... Tom.

We (7) ..... for a house for weeks but we still (8) ..... anything. So you see, I (9) ..... quite busy lately too!

Anyway, I'll see you when you're back from Spain. Have a wonderful time and send me a postcard from Madrid, (10) ..... you?

Love,

Julia

0	a take	b taking	c 're taking	d taken
1	a deserve	b 're deserving	c 've deserved	d 've been deserving
2	a work	b 're working	c works	d 've been working
3	a don't go	b doesn't go	c aren't going	d haven't been going
4	a think	b 're thinking	c thinks	d thinking
5	a don't like	b 'm not liking	c haven't liked	d haven't been liking
6	a has	b does	c hasn't	c doesn't
7	a look	b 're looking	c 've looked	d 've been looking
8	a don't find	b aren't finding	c haven't found	d haven't been finding
9	a am	b do	c 've been	d been
10	a will	b do	c are	d have

10

2 Rewrite the sentences using the word given.

0 He hasn't called me since Monday.
The last ...time he called me was... on Monday. **time**

1 I last visited my grandparents a month ago.
I .... for a month. **not**

2 We haven't gone out for two weeks. **last**
We .... two weeks ago.

3 Dawn started working here a year ago. **has**
Dawn .... for a year.

4 They last had a meeting in November. **since**
They haven't .... November.

5 I haven't been to that restaurant for years. **was**
The last time I .... years ago.

10

3 Rewrite the sentences using the words given.

0 I went to bed and then my parents came home. **already**
   I ___had already gone to bed___ when my parents came home.

1 He finished his homework and then he watched TV. **after**
   He watched TV .... his homework.

2 It was the first time I had ever eaten Mexican food. **never**
   I .... Mexican food before.

3 She left the office and John arrived later. **already**
   She .... when John arrived.

4 I had never heard such a funny story before. **ever**
   It was the first time .... such a funny story.

5 I finished my breakfast and then I started cleaning the house. **soon**
   As .... my breakfast, I started cleaning the house.

(10)

4 Circle the correct answer.

0 We were having lunch when we (heard)/ were hearing a terrible noise.
1 The bus *had left* / *had been leaving* by the time we got to the station.
2 I finally finished that report. I *have been working* / *had been working* on it for weeks.
3 The play *finished* / *had finished* by 10.30.
4 I *ran* / *was running* into Daniella as I was walking to school.
5 They *lived* / *have lived* in that house since 1990.
6 That building *used to be* / *would be* a hotel.
7 No, Julian isn't at home. He *has been* / *has gone* to the market.
8 We were sitting in the garden while Mum *was making* / *made* dinner.
9 I *called* / *used to call* him ten minutes ago.
10 We *already had* / *'ve already had* lunch, thank you.

(10)

5 Read and complete. Use only one word in each space.

A New World Record?

In 1996 Kenichi Hori made the fastest ever crossing of the Pacific Ocean. It took him 148 days to cross it in a solar-powered boat.

But David Powell, a twenty-eight-year-old man from Bristol, thinks he can break this record. He is going (0) ___to___ cross the Pacific Ocean in a small boat and he hopes that he (1) .... set a new world record. 'I expect I (2) .... complete my journey in 145 days. When I come back, I am (3) .... to throw the biggest party ever! After all, my dream will (4) .... come true,' David told me.

David (5) .... leaving Bristol on Friday. He will (6) .... travelling in a solar-powered boat, just like Kenichi Hori. He hopes he will (7) .... returned by the end of October. (8) .... the time he comes back, he will have (9) .... travelling for more than five months.

Well, what can we say? We all hope that David's dream (10) .... come true.

Good luck, David!

(10)

Total (50)

37

Modals (1)

ability, permission, requests, offers, suggestions

5

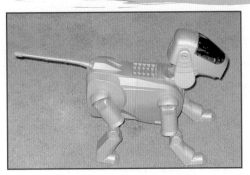

Teen Link

The American International Toy Fair

By Isabella Hicks

A few months ago, toy shop owners **were able to** see thousands of new toys at the American International Toy Fair in New York City. These toys were amazing but unfortunately, many of them were also top secret! Visitors **weren't allowed to** take photos of these, so we **couldn't** get pictures to show you. But we **can** tell you that they are very exciting, especially the robotic toys. Some of these **are able to** eat, sleep and do really incredible things.

If, like me, you are dying to see or buy them, don't worry! You **will** soon **be able to** see them yourself at your local toy shops.

Grammar reference

A | **Ability**

Can
▶ We use **can** to express ability (capability) in the present or the future.
He can speak Italian.
We can't meet them tomorrow.
Can you hear a noise outside?

Could
▶ **Could** is the past simple of **can**. It expresses ability in the past.
Wanda could walk when she was only nine months old.

Be able to

▶ Can has only two forms: **can** (present simple) and **could** (past simple). We use **be able to** in the other tenses.

Present simple	They **are able to** talk.
Past simple	They **were able to** talk.
Future	They **will be able to** talk.
Present perfect	They **have been able to** talk.

▶ **Be able to** may be used like **can** to express ability in the present and future. **Can** is used more often though.
She can speak four languages.
She is able to speak four languages.

We can't come to your party next week.
We won't be able to come to your party next week.

Could and was/were able to

▶ To describe a general ability in the past, we can either use **could** or **was/were able to.**
Keith could play the piano when he was six.
Keith was able to play the piano when he was six.

▶ But to describe somebody's ability in a particular situation in the past, ie. what somebody managed to do, we only use **was/were able to**, but not **could.**
Firefighters were able to get everybody out of the burning building last night.
~~**Firefighters could get everybody out of the burning building last night.**~~ ✗

▶ In negative sentences, **couldn't** and **wasn't/weren't able** may also be used for a general ability and for an ability in a particular situation in the past.
The man was very old, so he couldn't walk fast. (general ability)
The man was very old, so he wasn't able to walk fast. (general ability)

We queued for hours but we couldn't get tickets for the concert. (particular situation)
We queued for hours but we weren't able to get tickets for the concert. (particular situation)

Grammar practice

I Complete with the correct form of *be able to*.

1 Sarah _was able to_ write when she was five.

2 We had our cameras with us, so we .... take some photographs.

3 .... you .... help me clean the garage tomorrow?

4 I .... sing since I was a child.

5 Nobody called the police, so the thieves .... escape.

6 Our car broke down but we .... repair it ourselves.

7 We .... come to your party next week. We're too busy.

8 .... you .... visit your grandparents every weekend?

9 She .... run faster a few years ago.

10 I've been so busy that I .... visit them for weeks.

2 Complete with *could, couldn't, was/were able to* or *wasn't/weren't able to*. In some sentences, more than one answer is possible.

1 I _could / was able to_ read when I was five.

2 He .... play in the match because he had broken his leg.

3 We didn't have our keys but we .... get in through the kitchen window.

4 She spoke too fast. I .... understand what she was saying.

5 I finished my homework early last night and so I .... go to bed early.

6 He .... dance really well when he was younger.

7 I knew I had seen him before but I .... remember his name.

8 She didn't speak French well but she .... understand what people said.

9 The detective found some new clues and in the end he .... solve the mystery.

10 The child tried and tried but she .... do it.

B Permission

Can, could, may
▶ To ask for somebody's permission to do something, we can use **can**, **could** or **may**. **Could** is more polite than **can**, while **may** is more formal.
Can I use your phone?
Could I use your phone?
May I use your phone?

▶ To give somebody permission to do something, we use **can** or **may** (but not **could**).
May is more formal.
You can borrow my camera.
You may borrow my camera.

▶ To refuse somebody permission for something, we use **can't** and **may not**.
You can't park here.
You may not park here.

▶ **Couldn't** is not used to refuse permission for something.
–Could I use your phone?
–I'm afraid you can't.
– I'm afraid you couldn't. ✗

Be allowed to
▶ To refer to rules and more generally, to what is and is not allowed, we use **can**, **could** and **be allowed to**.

▶ To talk about the present or the future, we use **can** or **be allowed to**.
Students can use the library on Mondays and Fridays.
Students are allowed to use the library on Mondays and Fridays.

Can we leave school early tomorrow?
Will we be allowed to leave school early tomorrow?

▶ To talk about something that was generally allowed in the past, we use **could** or
I couldn't stay up late when I was eleven.
I wasn't allowed to stay up late when I was eleven.

▶ But if we want to talk about something that we were allowed to do in a particular situation in the past, we only use **was/were allowed to**, but not **could**.
I was allowed to stay up late last night.
I could stay up late last night. ✗

3 Complete with the correct form of *be allowed to*.

1 Put that cigarette out! You <u>aren't allowed to</u> smoke in here! ✗

2 We visited the museum but we .... take any photos. ✗

3 .... we .... see the plans tomorrow?

4 We .... usually .... stay up late on Saturdays. ✓

5 When I was a student, we .... wear jeans at school. ✗

6 Remember, you .... use your dictionaries during the exam tomorrow. ✗

7 Visitors .... feed the animals at the zoo. ✗

8 In some countries you .... drive if you're over sixteen. ✓

4 Rewrite the sentences using the word given.

1 We are allowed to turn left here. (can)
<u>We can turn left here.</u>

2 Can I use the equipment? (allowed)
....

3 People aren't allowed to bring sandwiches into the library. (can't)
....

4 Can you eat and drink in a museum? (allowed)
....

5 He isn't allowed to use his computer in the aeroplane. (can't)
....

6 You can look at your test papers now. (allowed)
....

7 Are we allowed to take our dog into the restaurant? (can)
....

8 We can feed the ducks at the lake. (allowed)
....

5 Ask for permission in the following situations.

☺ = polite
☺☺ = very polite
☺☺☺ = extremely polite

Tip

Could is more polite than can.
May is more formal and polite than can and could.

1 You're at a friend's house and you'd like to use the phone. Ask your friend. ☺
<u>Can I use your phone?</u>

2 You're in a library and you need to borrow a pen. A boy sitting next to you has got one. Ask him. ☺☺
....

3 You'd like to go to the cinema tonight. Ask your parents. ☺
....

4 You're on a bus, it's hot and the window's closed. Ask the driver. ☺☺☺
....

5 You're in a clothes shop and you'd like to try on a shirt. Ask the shop assistant. ☺☺
....

6 You're having an English lesson but you'd like to leave class early. Ask your teacher. ☺☺☺
....

7 It's your birthday next week and you'd like to have a party on Saturday. Ask your parents. ☺☺
....

C Requests

▶ To ask somebody to do something for us, we can use **can**, **could**, **will** or **would**. Could and would are more formal and polite.
Can you help me?
Will you carry this bag for me?
Could you open the window?
Would you post these letters?

▶ To ask for something from somebody, we can use **Can/Could/May I ... ?**
But we cannot use
Will/would I ...?
Can I have some water?
Could I speak to Mr Jones?
May I use your pen?

6 Make requests using the words given.

1 wash the dishes
2 feed the cats
3 make the beds
4 call my boss
5 go to the supermarket
6 cook something for lunch
7 water the plants
8 call the doctor

1	(could)	Could you wash the dishes?
2	(will)	
3	(can)	
4	(would)	
5	(will)	
6	(would)	
7	(could)	
8	(can)	

7 Make requests in the following situations.

1 You're carrying some books and you can't open the door. Ask your friend to open it for you.
Can you open the door for me?

2 You're at a friend's house and you're thirsty. Ask your friend's mother for a glass of water.
....

3 You're trying to sleep but your brother is making a noise. Ask him to be quiet.
....

4 You're in bed. You're cold and the window's open. Ask your sister to close it.
....

5 You're trying to do an exercise but you can't. Ask your teacher to help you.
....

6 You call a friend but he/she isn't at home. Ask his/her mother to give him/her a message.
....

7 Your friend has come to pick you up but you aren't ready. Ask him/her to wait for five minutes.
....

D | Offers

There are many ways to offer to do something for somebody.

I'll ...	I'll help you with that suitcase.
Shall I ...?	Shall I help you with that suitcase?
Can I ...?	Can I help you with that suitcase?
Could I ...?	Could I help you with that suitcase?
Would you like me to ...?	Would you like me to help you with that suitcase?
Would you like ...?*	Would you like a cup of tea?

* With **Would you like + noun**, we are not offering to do something for somebody but we are offering something to somebody.

8 Complete with *Shall I ...?* or *I'll ...* and a verb from the box.

| carry   get   open   switch   lend   go   help |

1 A: It's hot.
B: Shall I open .... the window?

2 A: I haven't got enough money to buy this book.
B: .... you some.

3 A: I'm thirsty.
B: .... you some water?

4 A: It's dark in here.
B: .... on the light?

5 A: I can't do this exercise.
B: .... you.

6 A: We need some bread.
B: .... to the baker's?

7 A: These books are too heavy.
B: .... them for you.

9 Complete with *Would you like ...?* or
Would you like me to ...?

1 *Would you like* .... some tea?
2 *Would you like me to* ... pour you another cup
 of tea?
3 .... a cheese sandwich?
4 .... pass you the salt?
5 .... hold that for you?
6 .... another slice of cake?
7 .... drive you to the airport?
8 .... a glass of water?

E **Suggestions**

There are many ways of suggesting
something to somebody.

Shall we ...?	Shall we go out tonight?
We can/could ...	We can/could go out tonight.
How about ...?	How about going out tonight?
What about ...?	What about going out tonight?
Why don't we ...?	Why don't we go out tonight?

---

10 Complete with the correct form of the verb.

Nancy: It's late. What about (1) ...*getting*... (get)
 dinner ready?

Mark: Yes, I'm hungry. Shall we (2) ....
 (make) a pizza?

Francis: We could (3) .... (order) one
 from the takeaway.

Nancy: Well, yes, we could. But home-made
 pizza is tastier. How about (4) ....
 (help) me? Francis, what about
 (5) .... (lay) the kitchen table?

Mark: Why don't we (6) .... (have)
 dinner outside on the balcony? It's a
 lovely evening.

Nancy: Good idea.

11 Rewrite the sentences using the word
given.

1 Why don't we watch TV? **about**
 How ...*about watching*... TV?
2 I couldn't sleep last night. **able**
 I .... last night.
3 Shall I carry that bag for you? **like**
 Would .... that bag for you?
4 What about inviting Larry to the party? **we**
 Why .... Larry to the party?
5 I'd like some more coffee. **have**
 Could .... some more
 coffee?
6 It's against the law to drive without a
 licence. **allowed**
 You .... without a licence.
7 We couldn't find a room at the hotel. **to**
 We .... a room at the hotel.
8 Why don't we listen to some music? **we**
 Shall .... to some music?
9 My parents said I couldn't go to Jill's party
 last week. **allow**
 My parents didn't .... to Jill's
 party last week.
10 Would you like me to get you some tea? **I**
 Shall .... some tea?
11 Joanna pushed the door but she couldn't
 open it. **able**
 Joanna pushed the door but she
 .... it.
12 Children can't use the equipment without
 permission. **to**
 Children .... the equipment
 without permission.
13 Shall we cook dinner tonight? **us**
 Would .... dinner tonight?
14 I'm bored. What about going to the cinema?
 we
 I'm bored. Why .... to the
 cinema?

Writing practice Now you can do the **writing activity** for **Unit 5** (Teacher's Resource File).

Modals (2)
obligation and necessity, absence of obligation, prohibition/restriction, advice/advisability/criticism, possibility, probability, deduction

TeenLink

Study Tips
by Leslie Banks

Are you fed up with studying? If the answer is 'yes', you **ought to** change your study habits. Here are some tips that **might** help you.
- You **need to** find a good place to study. It **should** be quiet and comfortable.
- You **must** keep your study area organised and tidy. Then you **won't have to** spend hours looking for your books.
- You **should** take a break every hour.

- You **mustn't** panic if there's a lot to do. Plan your work and don't waste time.
- Finally, a good student **has to** be healthy. Get lots of sleep and eat healthy food!

Grammar reference

A **Obligation and necessity**
Form

	Affirmative	Question
must		
Present/Future	She **must** try hard.	**Must** she try hard?
have to		
Present/Future	She **has to** try hard.	**Does** she **have to** try hard?
Past simple	She **had to** try hard.	**Did** she **have to** try hard?
Future	She **will have to** try hard.	**Will** she **have to** try hard?
Present perfect	She **has had to** try hard.	**Has** she **had to** try hard?
need to		
Present/Future	She **needs to** try hard.	**Does** she **need to** try hard?
Past simple	She **needed to** try hard.	**Did** she **need to** try hard?
Future	She **will need to** try hard.	**Will** she **need to** try hard?
Present perfect	She **has needed to** try hard.	**Has** she **needed to** try hard?

Use

▶ We use **must** and **have to** to express obligation. **Must** is only used for the present and the future.
I must get up at six o'clock every day.
I must write a letter to Jake tomorrow.

▶ **Have to** may be used in all of the tenses.
I have to get up at six o'clock on weekdays. (present)
I had to get up at six o'clock yesterday. (past)
I'll have to get up at six o'clock tomorrow. (future)
Have you ever had to get up at six o'clock on a Sunday? (present perfect)

▶ **Have got to** is used in the same way as **have to**. We usually use it in oral speech.
We've got to do our homework.
We have to do our homework.

Have we got to do our homework?
Do we have to do our homework?

▶ In the negative, **must** and **have to** are used to express obligation. They have another meaning. (See tables B (Absence of obligation) and C (Prohibition/Restriction)).

▶ **Must** is used to express an obligation that the speaker himself feels he has, ie. that he is imposing upon himself. **Have to** is used to express an obligation that is imposed by some other factor, eg. by a person, a situation or by rules.
I must go to bed. I feel really tired.
I have to be at work early tomorrow because my boss wants to see me.

▶ We use **need to** to express necessity.
We need to clean the garage.

B **Absence of obligation**

▶ To refer to something that is not necessary, something that does not need to happen, we can use:
- **don't have to + infinitive**
You don't have to get up early tomorrow.
- **don't need to + infinitive**
You don't need to get up early tomorrow.
- **needn't + infinitive without 'to'**
You needn't get up early tomorrow.

▶ To talk about something that did not need to happen in the past, we can use:
- **didn't have to + infinitive**
He didn't have to go to work yesterday.

- **didn't need to + infinitive**
He didn't need to go to work yesterday.
- **needn't have + past participle**
He needn't have gone to work yesterday.

▶ We use **didn't have to, didn't need to** to refer to an action which we already knew from the past was not necessary. We usually mean that this action finally did not take place.
I didn't have to/didn't need to get up early, so I stayed in bed.

▶ With **needn't have + past participle** we refer to an action that was not necessary but took place.
You needn't have hurried. We had plenty of time.

C **Prohibition/Restriction**

We can use **mustn't, can't** or **not allowed to** to express prohibition or restriction
You mustn't touch the paintings.
We can't park here.
You aren't allowed to talk during the exam.

6

Grammar practice

1 Complete with the correct form of *have to*.

1 I was late for work, so I ......had to...... take a taxi.

2 She's a nurse, so she .... wear a uniform at work.

3 We .... go to the supermarket tomorrow. There's no time today.

4 He didn't feel well, so we .... call a doctor.

5 She .... wear glasses since she was four years old.

6 He's a police officer. He often .... work at night.

7 It's getting late. We .... leave soon.

8 She's ill. She .... stay in bed since last week.

2 Form questions using *have to*.

1 A: He had to go somewhere.
   B: Where *did he have to go?* ....

2 A: I have to meet someone at one o'clock.
   B: Who ....

3 A: We'll have to get up early.
   B: What time ....

4 A: She had to leave.
   B: Why ....

5 A: I have to see a doctor.
   B: Why ....

6 A: They had to be somewhere at seven.
   B: Where ....

7 A: We will have to hurry!
   B: Why ....

8 A: She has had to cancel her appointment.
   B: Why ....

3 Circle the correct answer.

Tip

Remember:
Must expresses an obligation that the speaker is imposing upon himself.
With **have to**, we refer to an obligation that somebody else is imposing upon the speaker.

1 I *must /* (*have to*) be at the office at eight o'clock every day.

2 I *must / have to* put a new film in my camera. I want to take some pictures.

3 In Britain you *must / have to* drive on the left.

4 I *must / have to* start working harder. I'd like to improve my marks at school.

5 You *must / have to* get a new passport if you want to travel to the USA.

6 We *must / have to* wear a uniform at work.

7 I *must / have to* hurry. I don't want to be late.

8 I *must / have to* finish this report today. The boss will be very angry if I don't.

9 You *must / have to* read this book. It's excellent!

10 I really *must / have to* phone Fiona. I haven't spoken to her for ages!

4 Read the sentences below. Some are correct and some have a word which should not be there. If a sentence is correct, put a tick next to it. If a sentence has a word which should not be there, write the word at the end of the line.

1 I have to work late on Mondays. ....✓

2 You mustn't ~~to~~ touch the red button. ....to...

3 We've got to do something about this. ....

4 You must to come and see us when you visit London. ....

5 We need to start looking for a new flat. ....

6 You don't have got to ring the bell. I have a key. ....

7 You don't needn't hurry. ....

8 I can't to hear you. ....

9 Are we allowed to take photos in here? ....

10 You don't need to get up early tomorrow. ....

11 He didn't need to ask us. ....

12 They needn't to have spent so much money. ....

13 She must see the exhibition. ....

14 You needn't worry. Everything will be all right. ....

5 Complete with *mustn't* or *don't have to.*

Tip

Remember:
Mustn't expresses prohibition.
Don't have to refers to something that is not necessary.

1 You .don't have to.. wait for me. I can meet you later.

2 We .... make any noise when we go inside. Everyone's asleep.

3 Hurry up! We .... be late!

4 You .... leave yet. You can stay a bit longer.

5 I .... forget to call Tim. It's very important.

6 She .... go to school tomorrow. It's the weekend.

7 We .... do this now. It can wait.

8 You .... tell anyone about it. It's a secret.

9 You .... touch that! It's dangerous!

10 You .... wash the car. I washed it yesterday.

11 Hey! You .... walk on the grass. Look at that sign.

12 You .... eat in the library. It isn't allowed.

6 Complete with *didn't need to* or *needn't have* and the correct form of the verb.

Tip

We use **didn't need to + infinitive** for an action that was not necessary and that did not take place.
We use **needn't have + past participle** for an action that took place despite the fact that it was not necessary

1 I _didn't need to wake_ (wake) her. She was already in the shower.

2 She .... (stay) at the office, so she came home early.

3 Thank you for the flowers but you really .... (buy) so many.

4 Why didn't you take the bus? You .... (walk) home.

5 Pamela gave the children a lift, so they .... (walk) to school today.

6 You .... (borrow) Dave's bike. You could have used mine.

7 He didn't go to the supermarket because he .... (buy) anything.

8 We .... (prepare) so much food. Now we'll have to throw some of it away.

9 The students .... (be) worried about the test. It was easier than they had expected.

10 Nora gave me a free ticket, so I .... (queue) to buy one.

D | **Advice/Advisability/Criticism**

Form

	Affirmative	Question	Negative
should			
Present/Future	They **should tell** him.	**Should** they **tell** him?	They **should not (shouldn't) tell** him.
Past	They **should have told** him.	**Should** they **have told** him?	They **should not (shouldn't) have told** him.
ought to			
Present/Future	They **ought to tell** him.	**Ought** they **to tell** him?	They **ought not to (oughtn't to) tell** him.
Past	They **ought to have told** him.	**Ought** they **to have told** him?	They **ought not to (oughtn't to) have told** him.

	Affirmative		Negative	
had better	You **had better** (You'd better) **tell** him.		You **had better** (You'd better) **not tell** him.	

D **Use**

▶ To give advice to somebody or more generally, to say what we consider is right (advisability), we can use **should**, **ought to** and **had better**. **Should** and **ought to** are used in the same way.
You should visit your dentist twice a year for a check-up.
You ought to visit your dentist twice a year for a check-up.

▶ With **had better**, we often warn somebody about something immediate. We mean that if he does not follow the advice that we are giving, a problem may arise.
–My tooth hurts.
–You'd better go to the dentist.

▶ We use **should/ought to** + **have** + **past participle** to refer to something that we believe should have happened differently in the past from what finally happened (criticism).
You should have been more careful. (But you weren't.)

7 Complete with *should, shouldn't, ought* or *oughtn't*.

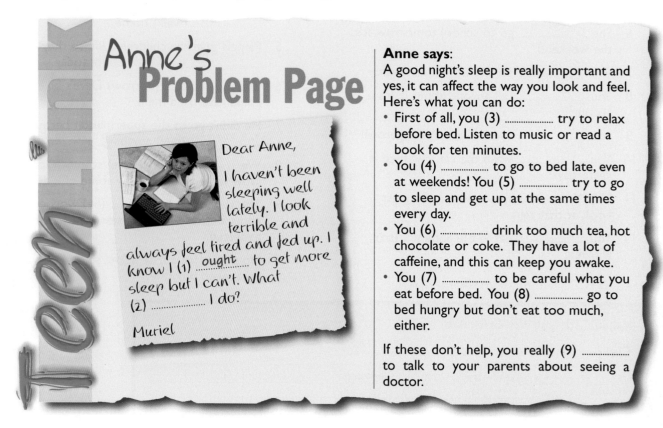

Anne's Problem Page

Dear Anne,

I haven't been sleeping well lately. I look terrible and always feel tired and fed up. I know I (1) __ought__ to get more sleep but I can't. What (2) _____ I do?

Muriel

Anne says:
A good night's sleep is really important and yes, it can affect the way you look and feel. Here's what you can do:

• First of all, you (3) .... try to relax before bed. Listen to music or read a book for ten minutes.

• You (4) .... to go to bed late, even at weekends! You (5) .... try to go to sleep and get up at the same times every day.

• You (6) .... drink too much tea, hot chocolate or coke. They have a lot of caffeine, and this can keep you awake.

• You (7) .... to be careful what you eat before bed. You (8) .... go to bed hungry but don't eat too much, either.

If these don't help, you really (9) .... to talk to your parents about seeing a doctor.

8 Form sentences using *had better*.

1 It's cold. (you / put on / a coat)
   You had better put on a coat.

2 You don't look very well. (you / not go / to school today)
   ....

3 It's 10.30! (we / hurry)
   ....

4 Mike will be waiting for us at the bus stop. (we / not be / late)
   ....

5 Look at those clouds! (you / take / an umbrella / with you)
   ....

6 There's someone in the house. (we / call / the police)
   ....

7 That dog is dangerous. (you / not go / near it)
   ....

8 What a mess! (you / tidy / your room)
   ....

9 Rewrite the sentences using the words given.

1 Why didn't you call me last night? (should)
You should have called me last night.

2 Why were you so rude to her? (shouldn't)
You ....

3 Why didn't he tell me about this? (ought)
He ....

4 Why didn't you leave her a note? (should)
You ....

5 Why did she invite Mike to the party? (shouldn't)
She ....

6 Why didn't we bring the map? (ought)
We ....

7 Why weren't you more careful with that vase? (ought)
You ....

8 Why did you read my diary? (shouldn't)
You ....

10 Complete with *might* or *might have* and the correct form of the verb.

1 A: I can't find my purse.
  B: It ......might be...... (be) in the car.

2 A: I can't find my purse.
  B: You .... (leave) it in the car.

3 A: Where are the children?
  B: I don't know. They .... (be) in the garden.

4 A: I wonder why Frank hasn't called.
  B: Well, he .... (forget).

5 A: Why didn't she come to the party?
  B: I don't know. She .... (be) busy.

6 A: Have you decided about the picnic tomorrow?
  B: No, I'm not sure yet. I .... (not come) with you.

7 A: Kevin wasn't at school yesterday.
  B: He .... (be) ill.

8 A: I wonder where Tom is.
  B: He .... (go) shopping.

9 A: I saw Helen but she didn't say hello.
  B: Well, she .... (not see) you.

10 A: Do you know where Alex is?
   B: Ask Sarah. She .... (know).

E **Possibility**

▶ We can use **could, may** or **might** to express possibility in the present or future.
Jim is not at the office. He could be at home.

▶ In negative sentences, we can use **may not** or **might not**, but not **couldn't**.
I may/might not come with you tomorrow.
~~I couldn't come with you tomorrow.~~ ✗

▶ To refer to the past, we use **could/may/might have + past participle.**
Jim is not here. He may have gone home.

F **Probability**

▶ We use **should/ought to** to refer to something that is particularly possible or expected to happen (**probability**) in the present or future.

Jane should be here any minute now.

▶ We use **should/ought to + have + past participle** to refer to something that was particularly possible or expected to take place in the past.
The train ought to have arrived five minutes ago.

---

11 Rewrite the sentences using the word given.

USE OF FCE ENGLISH

1 Perhaps he's in his room. **could**
He ......could be...... in his room.

2 Perhaps she'll lend us the money. **might**
She .... the money.

3 Perhaps he missed the bus. **could**
He .... the bus.

4 Perhaps she has already heard the news. **might**
She .... the news.

5 Perhaps they'll come with us. **may**
They .... with us.

6 Perhaps he forgot about the meeting. **could**
He .... the meeting.

7 Perhaps she lost her way. **may**
She .... her way.

8 Perhaps he's too busy to call. **could**
He .... too busy to call.

12 Complete with *should* or *ought*.

1 The report ....*should*.... be ready by ten.

2 The plane .... have arrived by now.

3 They .... to win the game easily.

4 You .... not have any problems with this exercise.

5 He .... to be at home by now.

6 Jack .... to finish work earlier today.

7 She .... to have got your message by now.

G | **Deduction**

▶ We use **must** and **can't** to express a logical conclusion (**deduction**). Must expresses a positive conclusion. **Can't** expresses a negative conclusion.
He's been working all day. He must be tired.
She can't be at home. I saw her here a few seconds ago.

▶ We use **must/can't + have + past participle** to refer to the past.
I didn't hear the phone. I must have been asleep.
You can't have seen a ghost!

---

13 Complete with *must, must have, can't, can't have* and the correct form of the verb.

1 You ....*can't be*.... (be) hungry! You've just had three sandwiches!

2 He .... (be) tired. He got out of bed twenty minutes ago.

3 They .... (be) at the theatre last night. They moved to Australia a year ago!

4 David's late. He .... (miss) the bus.

5 They .... (arrive) in Paris. They only left London half an hour ago.

6 That .... (be) Linda's brother. He looks a lot like her.

7 That looks like Kate but it .... (be) her. Kate's got blue eyes.

8 He's got thousands of CDs. He .... (love) music.

9 She .... (be) tired. She hasn't had any sleep for nearly two days.

---

10 You .... (pay) £500 for this ring! It's not gold!

11 She didn't call me. She .... (fall) asleep.

12 Their car is parked outside their house. They .... (be) at home.

---

14 Rewrite the sentences using the word given.

USE OF FCE ENGLISH

1 I'm almost sure that wasn't Jane. **have**
That ....*can't have been*.... Jane.

2 You are not allowed to enter this room. **must**
You .... this room.

3 It wasn't necessary for you to buy all these books. **bought**
You .... all these books.

4 It wasn't right that you talked to her like that. **should**
You .... to her like that.

5 You should look for a better job. **ought**
You .... for a better job.

6 Perhaps she's at the office. **might**
She .... at the office.

7 It isn't necessary for her to wear a uniform at school. **have**
She .... a uniform at school.

8 You don't have to cook lunch today. **need**
You .... lunch today.

9 It's possible that they got lost. **might**
They .... lost.

10 I'm sure they have gone out. **must**
They .... out.

11 If I were you, I would visit Japan instead of China. **should**
You .... Japan instead of China.

12 I really think you should work harder. **better**
You .... harder.

15 Read the text below. Some of the lines are correct and some have a word which should not be there. If a line is correct, put a tick next to it. If a line has a word which should not be there, write the word at the end of the line.

TeenLink
Keeping Fit

You ~~are~~ definitely have to exercise for lots of reasons. We all	1	...are...
should keep our bodies strong and healthy. But some of us	2	....
may does not like organised sports. Others might be too busy.	3	....
Well, you don't have got to worry. There are lots of activities	4	....
you can do. You needn't to be a sporty person to keep fit. The	5	....
key is doing something fun. You should be look for activities	6	....
that increase the blood circulation and make you sweat a little!	7	....
You don't to need to join a football team or go to the gym.	8	....
Dancing or riding your bike, for example, are great forms of	9	....
exercise. All you have better to do is find one that's right for you!	10	....

Oral practice   Now you can do the **oral activity** for **Unit 6** (Teacher's Resource File).

Conditionals
zero conditional, first conditional, second conditional, third conditional, mixed conditionals

'Thanks. If you hadn't warned me, I would have fallen.'

Grammar reference

A Form

Zero conditional (always)	
if/when + present simple – present simple	If it **doesn't rain**, the farmers **complain**. When the baby **is** hungry, she **cries**.
First conditional (present or future time)	
if + present simple – will + infinitive if + present simple – modal + infinitive if + present simple – imperative	If you **make** a noise, you**'ll wake** the neighbours. If those clothes **fit** him, he **can have** them. If you **leave** last, **switch off** the lights.
Second conditional (present or future time)	
if + past simple – would + infinitive if + past simple – modal + infinitive	If I **had** a pet, I **would be** so happy. If they **studied** harder, they **might get** better marks.
Third conditional (past time)	
if + past perfect – would + have + past participle if + past perfect – modal + have + past participle	If we **had followed** her, we **wouldn't have got** lost. If she **hadn't phoned** us, we **might** never **have found** out.
Mixed conditionals (past action, present result)	
if + past perfect – would/modal + infinitive	If I **hadn't been** so careless, I **wouldn't be** in trouble now.

▶ There are four basic types of conditional sentences. Each conditional sentence has two parts. The first part is the if clause, which starts with if and the second part is the main sentence, the main clause.

▶ The **if clause** can go at the beginning or at the end of the sentence. When the sentence starts with the **if clause**, the two parts of the sentence are separated by a comma. But when the **main clause** is before the **if clause**, we do not use a comma.
If I go to Italy, I'll send you a postcard.
I'll send you a postcard if I go to Italy.

B Zero conditional

Form
if/when + present simple – present simple

Often, we use **when** instead of if.
When you eat a lot, you get fat.

Use
We use the **zero conditional** when the if clause that we are making is based on actual facts or we are expressing general truths, states that always apply.
If you frighten the birds, they fly away.

C First conditional

Form

if + present simple – will + infinitive
if + present simple – modal + infinitive
if + present simple – imperative

In the **main clause** we can use:
▶ **will**
If I save up enough money, I will buy a new car.
▶ **modal verb** (eg can, may, might, must, have to, should, ought to)
If we aren't too busy, we might come with you.
▶ **Imperative**
If you see him, tell him about the party.

Use
We use the **first conditional** to refer to something that it is possible may happen in the present or in the future.
If she invites me to her party, I'll go.
If it stops raining, we can go shopping.

if and unless

We can use **unless** instead of if **not**.

I'll come and see you tomorrow if I'm not busy.
I'll come and see you tomorrow unless I'm busy.

Mum will be angry if I don't tidy my room.
Mum will be angry unless I tidy my room.

Provided (that), providing (that), as long as, so long as

The phrases **provided (that), providing (that), as long as** and **so long as** mean 'provided', 'as long as' and can be used in the **first conditional** instead of if.

If you promise to be careful, you can use my computer.
Provided (that) you promise to be careful, you can use my computer.
Providing (that) you promise to be careful, you can use my computer.
As long as you promise to be careful, you can use my computer.
So long as you promise to be careful, you can use my computer

Grammar practice

1 Form *zero conditional* sentences.

1 Jack / always / bring / flowers / when / he / come / to visit us
   <u>Jack always brings flowers when he comes to visit us.</u>

2 if / you / mix / red and blue / you / get purple
   ....

3 glass / break / when / you / heat / it?
   ....

4 if / you / not eat / you / get thin
   ....

5 when / the weather / be / nice / I / walk / to work
   ....

6 your brother / help / you / with your homework / when / he / have / time?
   ....

7 I / usually / read / a good book / when / I / not be / busy
   ....

8 if / plants / not get / enough water / they / die
   ....

2 Complete the *first conditional* sentences.

Mum will be angry if she sees this mess.

1 You ......<u>will feel</u>...... (feel) better if you ......<u>take</u>...... (take) an aspirin.

2 If they .... (come) with us, we .... (have) a great time.

3 If it .... (rain), I .... (might / stay) at home.

4 .... (you / post) this letter for me if you .... (not be) too busy?

5 You .... (should / apologise) if it .... (be) your fault.

6 If David .... (invite) Janice, I .... (not go) to his party.

7 If you .... (not know) the answer, ... (ask) Mr Walters.

8 Jock .... (move) to Scotland if he .... (find) a good job there.

9 If the pain .... (not stop), I .... (see) a doctor.

10 If you .... (not like) that dress, ... (not wear) it.

11 What .... (you / tell) Andrew if he .... (ask) you?

12 Prudence .... (can / borrow) her brother's car if she .... (ask) him nicely.

3 Rewrite the sentences using the word given.

Tip

Remember:
Unless means 'unless' and replaces **if not**.

1 You won't finish on time if you don't start now. (unless)
   <u>You won't finish on time unless you start now.</u>

2 Unless you read the instructions, you won't know what to do. (if)
   ....

3 We'll go to the cinema tonight if I'm not too tired. (unless)
   ....

4 Unless you study harder, you'll fail the test. (if)
   ....

5 If the neighbours don't stop making that awful noise, I'll call the police. (unless)
   ....

6 Mum won't let him go out if he doesn't finish his homework first. (unless)
   ....

7 The headache won't go away unless you do something about it. (if)
   ....

8 She won't hear you if you don't speak louder. (unless)
   ....

9 I'll be back at six unless I have to work late. (if)
   ....

10 He will never find a job unless he starts looking for one now. (if)
   ....

4 Rewrite the sentences using the word given.

1 I'll let you go to Philippa's house if you tidy your room. (provided)
   <u>I'll let you go to Philippa's house provided you</u>
   <u>tidy your room.</u>

2 Provided I finish work early tomorrow, I'll come with you. (if)
   ....

3 If you let me wear your sweater, I won't tell Mum what you did. (as long as)
   ....

4 Aunt Josephine will be here at eight as long as her train arrives on time. (providing)
   ....

5 You can borrow my car provided you bring it back at four. (as long as)
   ....

6 I'll go to the party as long as you come with me. (so long as)
   ....

7 If they offer him enough money, he will accept. (so long as)
   ....

8 I'll tell you all about it as long as you promise to keep it a secret. (providing)
   ....

D **Second conditional**

Form

if + past simple – would + infinitive
if + past simple – modal + infinitive

▶ In **second conditional** sentences, we can use **were** for all persons instead of **was** in the **if clause**.
If Archie was/were here, I'd tell him all about my problem.
If I was/were rich, I'd buy a house in Hollywood.

▶ In the **main clause**, apart from **would**, we can use a **modal verb** (eg. **could, might, should, ought to**).
If she were here, we could play chess together.

Use

We use the **second conditional**:
▶ to talk about something that does not apply to the present and when it is impossible that it will happen in the future.
If this ring was gold, I would sell it.

▶ to talk about something that does not apply to the present but could happen in the future.
If I met someone famous, I would ask them for an autograph.

▶ to give advice. In this case, we use the phrase **If I were you** in the if clause.
If I were you, I would buy a new car with that money.
If I were you, I wouldn't go near that dog.

---

5 Rewrite the sentences. Use the *second conditional.*

1 I haven't got any money, so I won't buy that CD.
   <u>If I had some money, I would buy that CD.</u>

2 Pigs haven't got wings, so they don't fly.
   ....

3 His marks aren't good because he doesn't work hard.
   ....

4 I'm busy, so I won't come with you.
   ....

5 They don't know her, so they won't invite her to their party.
   ....

6 I won't call him because I haven't got his phone number.
   ....

7 She walks to school because she hasn't got a bike.
   ....

8 It's cold, so we won't go to the beach.
   ....

9 I won't join you because I have to stay at home.
   ....

10 He won't lend you his camera because he needs it.
   ....

55

6 Read and complete.

Teen Link

Tricky ❀ ❀ ❀ ❀ ❀ situations: **what would _you_ do?**

What would you do if you found yourself in this tricky situation?

'You are looking through your parents' wedding album at the kitchen table when you accidentally spill some hot chocolate all over it.'

Here's what some of our readers would do:

If something like this (1) _happened_ (happen) to me, I (2) .... (hide) the album. But if my mum (3) .... (find) out, I (4) .... (admit) everything and apologise.

Christine, 15

If I (5) .... (spill) hot chocolate on the album, I (6) .... (try) to clean it off the photos and then I (7) .... (tell) my parents the truth. I'm sure they (8) .... (forgive) me if I (9) .... (be) honest.

Alaric, 13

If I (10) .... (ruin) my parents' wedding photos, I (11) .... (have to) leave the country!

Oliver, 16

---

7 Give advice using _If I were you_. Choose and write.

> ask her out   not eat so many sweets
> not watch so many horror films
> not work so hard   put on a jacket
> see a doctor   take an aspirin
> take up a hobby

1 Your friend hasn't been feeling well lately.
  If I were you, I would see a doctor.

2 Your sister wants to lose weight.
  ....

3 It's a cold afternoon. Your brother is leaving the house in a T-shirt.
  ....

4 Your elder sister finishes work at nine o'clock every night and she's always tired.
  ....

5 Your friend has a headache.
  ....

6 Your friend has been having nightmares recently.
  ....

7 Your brother really likes a new girl in his class but is too shy to speak to her.
  ....

8 Your little sister is bored at the weekends because she has nothing to do.
  ....

E Third conditional

Form

if + past perfect – would + have + past participle

if + past perfect – modal + have + past participle

▶ In the main clause, apart from would, we can use a modal verb (eg. could, might, should, ought to).

If you had warned me, I wouldn't have done it.

If they had caught the bus, they might not have missed the beginning of the film.

Use

We use the third conditional to refer to something that could have happened in the past but did not happen. Usually, with the third conditional, we express sorrow or regret about an event in the past.

If he had lent me the money, I would have bought that car.

If you hadn't told Mum about this, she wouldn't have got so upset.

8 Complete the *third conditional* sentences.

1 If I ....*had heard*...... (hear) the weather forecast, I *would have taken* (take) an umbrella with me.

2 If you .... (come) to the party last night, you .... (meet) James.

3 If I .... (listen) to her, this .... (not happen).

4 If I .... (know) you were at home, I .... (call) you.

5 What .... (you / do) if he .... (not lend) you his car?

6 If you .... (not be) so rude, she .... (not get) so upset.

7 If Raymond .... (not miss) the bus, he .... (not be) late for work.

8 If someone .... (tell) me that there was no milk in the house, I .... (go) to the supermarket.

9 She .... (not refuse) if you .... (ask) her nicely.

10 .... (you / come) with us if we .... (tell) you about the concert?

9 Rewrite the sentences. Use the *third conditional.*

1 I didn't say hello because I didn't see her.
If *I had seen her, I would have said hello.*

2 We didn't go out to dinner because Dad finished work late.
If ....

3 She was angry because you didn't call her.
If ....

4 We didn't hear about the accident because we didn't watch the news.
If ....

5 You dropped the vase because you weren't careful.
If ....

6 He didn't pass the exam because he was nervous.
If ....

7 We didn't go to the beach because it rained.
If ....

8 I had a good time because you were there with me.
If ....

9 They didn't get a taxi because they didn't have enough money.
If ....

10 We were late because our car broke down.
If ....

11 She didn't follow my advice, so she didn't make a profit.
If ....

12 You didn't put the milk in the fridge, so it went bad.
If ....

10 Rewrite the sentences. Use the *second* or *third conditional*.

> **Tip**
>
> With the **third conditional**, we refer to the past.
> With the **second conditional**, we refer to the present, to something that would apply now if something else happened.

1 She was ill, so she didn't go to school.
   If she hadn't been ill, she would have gone to school.

2 I haven't got a car, so I walk to work every morning.
   If ....

3 I didn't know it was her birthday, so I didn't buy her a present.
   If ....

4 You don't always tell him the truth, so he doesn't trust you.
   If ....

5 They don't work hard, so they do badly at school.
   If ....

6 The old man gave us clear directions, so we found the address.
   If ....

7 You don't get enough sleep, so you feel tired all the time.
   If ....

8 You forgot to bring a map, so we got lost.
   If ....

9 You didn't water the flowers, so they died.
   If ....

10 She trains hard, so she's a good player.
   If ....

11 Ms Dawson loves animals, so she has six cats.
   If ....

12 We didn't see them, so we didn't tell them about it.
   If ....

13 Max doesn't know about the subject, so he can't help.
   If ....

14 The critic didn't like the film, so she wrote a bad review.
   If ....

15 He likes children, so he gets on well with them.
   If ....

11 Read and complete.

Wendy: Hey, Kate. Are you coming to Rachel's house tonight?

Kate: Well, I would come if I (1) <u>didn't have</u> (not have) to look after my baby brother. My parents are going out tonight.

Wendy: Oh. Rachel (2) .... (be) disappointed if you don't come. She'd really like you to be there. It's her birthday, you know.

Kate: Her birthday? I didn't know it was her birthday! If I had known, I (3) .... (ask) my parents to get a baby sitter. Now they won't let me come unless they (4) .... (can / find) someone else to look after Bobby.

Wendy: You always look after Bobby when your parents (5) .... (go) out. Why don't you ask your sister to do it tonight?

Kate: Well, I (6) .... (ask) her if today wasn't so special for her. You see, she's going out with Peter. She'll be very angry if she (7) .... (have to) stay at home.

Wendy: Oh, well. If I (8) .... (be) you, I'd give it a try. Anyway, (9) .... (give) me a ring if you change your mind.

Kate: OK. I will. Bye.

F | **Mixed conditionals**

We can create conditional sentences by using the if clause from the **third conditional** and the main clause from the **second conditional**. This type of conditional sentence is called a **mixed conditional** and refers to the result that an action that happened in the past has in the present.

12 Match and write sentences.

1 If you had gone to bed earlier,
2 If Mum hadn't cooked dinner,
3 If you had been honest,
4 I would buy this book
5 You would know what to do
6 If Mary had taken that job six months ago,
7 I'd be in London right now
8 We wouldn't be in trouble
9 If I had bought that lottery ticket,
10 I would go to the party with Rita

a we would eat at a restaurant.
b she would not be unemployed today.
c if I hadn't already promised to go with Yvonne.
d if I hadn't spent all my money on CDs.
e if we had followed his advice.
f I would be rich today.
g you wouldn't be so tired.
h Dad wouldn't be so angry now.
i if I hadn't missed the bus.
j if you had listened to her instructions.

1 If you had gone to bed earlier, you wouldn't be so tired.
2 ....
3 ....
4 ....
5 ....
6 ....
7 ....
8 ....
9 ....
10 ....

13 Rewrite the sentences using the word given.

USE OF FCE ENGLISH

1 You should talk to William about this. **you**
   If I .... were you, I would talk .... to William about this.

2 She'll be very worried if I don't call her. **unless**
   She'll be very worried .... her.

3 We'll go fishing tomorrow if the weather is fine. **providing**
   We'll go fishing tomorrow .... fine.

4 You shouldn't stay up so late. **were**
   If ...., I wouldn't stay up so late.

5 She forgot to lock the door because she was in a hurry. **have**
   If she hadn't been in a hurry, she ....
   to lock the door.

6 I'll make dinner if you promise to wash the dishes. **provided**
   I'll make dinner .... to wash the
   dishes.

7 I'll read that article if I have nothing else to do tonight. **long**
   I'll read that article .... nothing else
   to do tonight.

8 She won't come to the party unless John invites her himself. **if**
   She won't come to the party .... her
   himself.

Oral practice   Now you can do the **oral activity** for **Unit 7** (Teacher's Resource File).

Wishes, 'It's time'

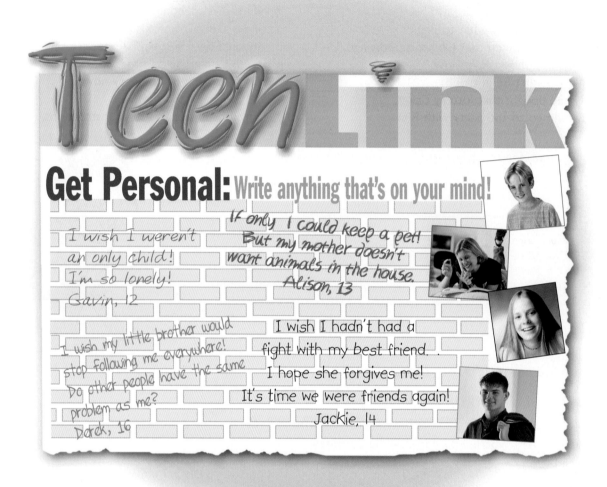

Get Personal: Write anything that's on your mind!

I wish I weren't an only child! I'm so lonely!
Gavin, 12

I wish my little brother would stop following me everywhere! Do other people have the same problem as me?
Derek, 16

If only I could keep a pet! But my mother doesn't want animals in the house.
Alison, 13

I wish I hadn't had a fight with my best friend. I hope she forgives me! It's time we were friends again!
Jackie, 14

Grammar reference

'Wishes'

A	Form	
	I wish/If only + past simple	I wish/If only I **had** a car.
	I wish/If only + would + infinitive	I wish/If only you **would stop** complaining!
	I wish/If only + past perfect	I wish/If only I **had taken** my camera with me.

B I wish/If only + past simple

▶ To make a wish for the present, to refer to something that we would like to be different, we use **I wish** or **If only** and the **past simple**. There is no substantial difference between **I wish** and **If only**. **If only** gives more emphasis to what we are saying.
I wish I knew the answer to that question.
If only we didn't have so much homework!
▶ When we use the verb **to be** with **I wish** or **If only**, we can use were instead of was.
I wish I was/were taller.
▶ Often, we use **could** after **I wish** and **If only**, to refer to an ability that we would like to have..
If only I could speak Italian!

C I wish/If only + would + infinitive

We use **would** after **I wish/If only** to complain about something, to express our desire to change a situation that is annoying us.
I wish you would stop making that noise!

D I wish/If only + past perfect

We use **I wish/If only** with the **past perfect** to express our sorrow about something that we would like to have happened differently in the past.
If only I had stayed at home last night!

Grammar practice

1 What do these people wish? Write sentences using the words given.

1 Barbara: I don't have an umbrella with me. (wish)
   I wish I had an umbrella with me.

2 Harry: I can't find my glasses anywhere! (if only)
   ....

3 Helen: I can't go to Jessica's party! (if only)
   ....

4 Steve: My job is so boring. (wish)
   ....

5 Martin: We have to go to school today. (if only)
   ....

6 Debbie: I am not old enough to drive. (wish)
   ....

7 Zacchary: I have to leave early. (if only)
   ....

8 Nora: I can't go home right now. (wish)
   ....

9 Kathy: That car is so expensive! (if only)
   ....

10 Carl: We live in the city centre. (if only)
    ....

11 Judy: I am not good at Maths. (wish)
    ....

12 Rory: I can't afford to buy my mother a nice present. (wish)
    ....

2 Write sentences using *would* and the prompts given.

1 Oh no! You've broken another glass! you / be / more careful (wish)
   I wish you would be more careful.

2 My little sister is always asking me questions. she / not bother / me all the time (if only)
   ....

3 George is so bossy! he / stop / telling me what to do (if only)
   ....

4 You talk too much. you / be / quiet (wish)
   ....

5 Mrs Edwards wants us to write another composition! she / not give / us so much homework (wish)
   ....

6 Bill and Fred are fighting again. they / stop / arguing (wish)
   ....

7 There's water everywhere! you / clean up / after your bath (if only)
   ....

8 Where's my blue sweater? you / not wear / my clothes without asking me first (wish)
   ....

9 My brother is so untidy! he / be / more careful with his things (if only)
   ....

10 My parents don't allow me to go out on weekdays. they / let / me go out with my friends (wish)
    ....

3 Write sentences using *wish* or *if only*.

1   We spent all our money on CDs.
    If only we hadn't spent all our money on CDs.

2   You didn't tell me the truth.
    I wish ....

3   I lost my car keys.
    I wish ....

4   I didn't listen to her.
    If only ....

5   We didn't win the game.
    I wish ....

6   I forgot to call him last night.
    If only ....

7   I failed the test.
    I wish ....

8   I was late for work.
    If only ....

9   Jim wasn't at the party last night.
    If only ....

10 I told her my secret.
    I wish ....

4 What does Alan wish? Complete with the correct form of the verb.

Tip

I wish/If only + past simple for the present or the future.
I wish/If only + past perfect for the past.

I wish I were on a tropical island right now.

1   If only I could find (can / find) a better job.

2   I wish I .... (work) harder when I was at school.

3   If only I .... (go) to university when I had had the chance.

4   I wish I .... (not have) to work.

5   I wish I .... (be) rich.

6   If only I .... (can / take) some time off work.

7   I wish I .... (not leave) my last job.

5 Write sentences using the prompts.

1   I don't know where she lives. I / have / her address – I / send / her an invitation
    I wish I had her address. If I had her address, I would send her an invitation.

2   I'd love to travel, but I'm broke. I / be / a millionaire – I / travel / around the world
    ....

3   We aren't allowed to go out tonight. we / not have to / stay / at home – we / go / bowling with our friends
    ....

4   I'm so lonely and bored here by myself. Jane / be / here with me – we / have / a great time
    ....

5   We only see each other a few times a year. he / not live / so far away – we / see / each other more often
    ....

6   We can only stay here for a few days. we / have / longer holidays – we / can relax / more
    ....

6 Write sentences using *I wish* and the *third conditional*.

1   I went to bed late last night. I was late for school this morning.
    I wish I hadn't gone to bed late last night. If I hadn't gone to bed late last night, I wouldn't have been late for school this morning.

2   I stayed in the sun for four hours. I got sunburnt.
    ....
    ....

3   I didn't study hard. I didn't pass the exam.
    ....
    ....

4   You didn't wake me up. I missed my plane.
    ....
    ....

5   I didn't give him my phone number. He didn't call me.
    ....
    ....

6   I was late. She was angry.
    ....
    ....

7   You didn't tell me about the exhibition. I didn't go.
    ....
    ....

'It's time'

E **It's time + subject + past simple**

We use the phrase **It's time** with the **past simple** to talk about something that we believe it is about time should happen or that should have already happened. Even if it is followed by the **past simple**, it does not refer to the past but to the present.
It's getting late. It's time we went home.
It's time you told him the truth.

7 Complete with *It's time* and the prompts.

1 I look awful! <u>It's time I had</u> (I / have) a haircut.

2 She's been working too hard lately. .... (she / take) some time off.

3 I'm tired. .... (I / go) to bed.

4 We have to be at the station at six. .... (we / leave).

5 .... (I / start) looking for a new job. I hate working in the city centre.

6 Those windows are very dirty. Don't you think .... (we / clean) them?

7 .... (you / buy) a new car. This one's too old.

8 What would you say in these situations? Write sentences using *It's time*.

1 Your brother has been watching TV for hours. He hasn't done his homework yet. <u>It's time you did your homework.</u>

2 You're at a friend's house. You promised to call your mother as soon as you got there but you haven't called her yet.
....

3 Your friend hasn't been feeling well lately. She hasn't seen a doctor yet.
....

4 Your room is in a terrible mess. You haven't tidied it for days.
....

5 Your father has to be at work at eight. It's half past seven and he's still sleeping.
....

6 You borrowed some money from a friend two weeks ago but you haven't paid him back yet.
....

9 Rewrite the sentences using the word given.

1 I would love to be at the beach right now. **were**
I ....<u>wish I were</u>........ at the beach right now.

2 What a pity I didn't bring my guitar. **wish**
I .... my guitar.

3 I want you to stop asking questions all the time. **would**
I .... asking questions all the time.

4 I'm really sorry but I can't answer your question. **wish**
I .... your question.

5 Unfortunately, we didn't visit the Acropolis when we were in Athens. **only**
If .... the Acropolis when we were in Athens.

6 I really think you should drive more carefully. **would**
I .... more carefully!

7 Unfortunately, I haven't got a driving licence. **wish**
I .... a driving licence.

8 It's a pity you didn't call us earlier. **only**
If .... us earlier.

9 I'd like to be rich and famous. **were**
I .... famous.

10 We should have gone to bed hours ago! **time**
It's .... to bed!

Writing practice Now you can do the **writing activity** for **Unit 8** (Teacher's Resource File).

Revision 5-8

1 Read and circle the correct answer.

Dear Tess,

I'm sorry I haven't been in touch for so long but I (0) ..d.. to do much these last two weeks. I've been busy getting ready for my trip. I'm flying to Paris, you know. (1) ..... me to get you anything?

I'm afraid I (2) ..... be able to meet you on Sunday morning. I'm driving my mum to the airport at eleven. But we (3) ..... go out together in the evening. (4) ..... going to see Hamlet? I went to the box office yesterday and I (5) ..... to get three tickets. (6) ..... we ask Carol to join us. I know she loves Shakespeare.

The play finishes at 9.30. (7) ..... have dinner at our favourite Italian restaurant afterwards? What do you think? (8) ..... you give me a ring on Monday?

Love,

Alice

PS I'll be working late on Monday, so (9) ..... call me at the office? You don't have to phone Carol. I'm going to see her at the office tomorrow, so (10) ..... tell her all about Sunday.

	a	b	c	d
0	couldn't	can't	'm not able	(d) haven't been able
1	Would you like	Do you like	Shall I	How about
2	can't	won't	couldn't	wouldn't
3	're able	're allowed	could	shall
4	Shall we	Would you like	Why don't we	How about
5	can	could	was able	would
6	We can	We would	How about	Why don't
7	We can	What about	How about	Why don't we
8	Shall	Will	May	Do
9	can you	may you	shall you	would you like
10	I'm able	I'm allowed	I'll	I would

(10)

2 Rewrite the sentences using the word given.

0   You mustn't read that message. **allowed**
    You _are not allowed to read_ that message.

1   That boy looks just like John, so I'm sure he's his brother. **must**
    That boy looks just like John, so he .... his brother.

2   Perhaps they went out. **might**
    They .... out.

3   Why didn't you tell me about this? **should**
    You .... me about this.

4   I really think you should start going to bed earlier. **better**
    You .... going to bed earlier.

5   You needn't do all the exercises. **have**
    You .... all the exercises.

(10)

3 Rewrite the sentences using the word given.

0   The pain won't go away unless you see a doctor. **if**
    The pain won't go away ....*if you don't see*........ a doctor.

1   I'll let you go to the party if you promise to be back by eleven. **provided**
    I'll let you go to the party .... to be back by eleven.

2   You should ask for help. **were**
    If ...., I would ask for help.

3   If we don't leave now, we'll be late for the meeting. **unless**
    We'll be late for the meeting .... now.

4   You had a stomach ache because you ate too much chocolate. **if**
    You wouldn't have had a stomach ache .... too much
    chocolate.

5   He doesn't go to the gym because he hasn't got much free time. **go**
    If he had more free time, ... to the gym.

(10)

4 Complete using the words given.

0   I didn't buy you a present. I wish .....*I had known*..... (I / know) it was your birthday.
1   I always make silly mistakes. I wish .... (I / not be) so careless.
2   I'll miss Jack. I wish .... (he / can / come) with us.
3   I feel really tired. If only .... (I / not stay) up late last night!
4   It's already seven thirty. It's time .... (you / do) your homework.
5   I have to take the bus to work. If only .... (I / have) a car!
6   My sweater shrank. I wish .... (I / not wash) it in hot water.
7   Mum will be back any minute now. It's time .... (you / tidy) your room.
8   I can't afford to buy that book. If only .... (I / save) the money Mum gave me last week!
9   I won't be able to join you. I wish .... (I / not have) to work next Sunday.
10   This house is too small. It's time .... (we / start) looking for a new one.

(10)

5 Read the sentences below. Some of the lines are correct and some have a
word which should not be there. If a line is correct put a tick ✓ next to it. If a
line has a word which should not be there, write the word at the end of the line.

0   I'm sure Brian would have spoken to you if he had seen you.   ....✓........
1   If you will see him, tell him I called.   ....
2   Would you like me to buy anything from the market?   ....
3   It's the time we went back home.   ....
4   You must to listen to the instructions very carefully.   ....
5   We needn't to hurry. It's only half past eight.   ....
6   I might have be a bit late tonight.   ....
7   If Fiona hadn't given me a lift, I would have missed my plane.   ....
8   I'll lend you the money providing you will pay me back by Friday.   ....
9   Unless we finish the project today, Mr Woods will be very angry.   ....
10   I wish only you had told me earlier.   ....

(10)

Total (50)

The Passive

Teen Link

A Fluffy Discovery
by Isabella Hicks

Was popcorn a Stone Age snack? Well, believe it or not, it was! It **is** now **believed** that cave people had popcorn.

Popcorn **was** first **grown** in Mexico, thousands of years before Columbus discovered America. Ancient popcorn seeds **have** recently **been discovered** in Peru. They **are thought to be** about 1,000 years old and they can still pop! Experts say that even popped popcorn **can be preserved** for long periods. Ancient popped popcorn **is** sometimes **found** in the South American deserts. And it still looks fresh and white when the sand and dust **is blown off** it! Now isn't that amazing?

Grammar reference

A

Form
subject + to be + past participle
▶ We form the passive voice using the verb to be in the tense that we need and the past participle of the main verb. See the table below.

	Active	Passive
Present simple	They **feed** the animals.	The animals **are fed**.
Present continuous	They **are feeding** the animals.	The animals **are being fed**.
Past simple	They **fed** the animals.	The animals **were fed**.
Past continuous	They **were feeding** the animals.	The animals **were being fed**.
Present perfect	They **have fed** the animals.	The animals **have been fed**.
Past perfect	They **had fed** the animals.	The animals **had been fed**.
will	They **will feed** the animals.	The animals **will be fed**.
Future perfect	They **will have fed** the animals.	The animals **will have been fed**.
going to	They **are going to feed** the animals.	The animals **are going to be fed**.
Modal verbs	They **must feed** the animals.	The animals **must be fed**.

▶ Often, in the **passive voice**, we usually use the verb **to get** instead of the verb **to be**. We usually use it in everyday speech to refer to something that happens by chance, suddenly or unexpectedly.
I got bitten by a dog on my way to school.

Use
▶ We use the **passive voice** when the action that we are talking about concerns us more than who did it or when we do not know who did this action.
This house was built in 1901.
Coffee is grown in Kenya.

Agent
▶ To say who did the action that we are talking about, ie. in order to refer to the agent, we add **by** and a name, noun or pronoun at the end of the sentence.
'Oliver Twist' was written by Charles Dickens.

▶ We do not refer to the **agent** when this is not important, when it is clear or when we do not know who did the action that we are talking about.
The missing boy was found two days ago.
The thieves haven't been arrested yet.
My bike was stolen last night.

▶ But when we want to state the material or object that was used for an action, we use **with**, not **by**.
The door was opened with a knife.
~~The door was opened by a knife.~~ ✗

Grammar practice

1 Complete with the *passive voice*. Use the tense given.

1 This film ___was directed___ (direct) by Sam Britton. (past simple)

2 English _____ (speak) all over the world. (present simple)

3 A new school _____ (build) in West Street. (present continuous)

4 Dinner _____ (serve) at 8.00. (will)

5 The rules _____ (must / obey) by all the students. (present simple)

6 The match _____ (cancel). (past perfect)

7 My car _____ (steal)! (present perfect)

8 The room _____ (clean) when I arrived. (past continuous)

2 Complete with the *passive voice*.

1 A space probe ___was sent___ (send) to Mars two months ago.

2 Roller skates _____ (invent) in 1949.

3 She _____ (might / interview) by a famous journalist.

4 The classrooms _____ (clean) every day.

5 We can't use my office at the moment. It _____ (clean).

6 I think a hospital _____ (build) here next year.

7 Mr Smith was waiting while his car _____ (repair).

8 We can't go to the concert. All the tickets _____ (sell).

9 I _____ (can / contact) in an emergency.

10 By the time the police arrived, all the money _____ (steal).

3 Form the negative and question.

Tulips are grown in Hawaii.

Really? Where are they grown?

You're wrong. They aren't grown in Hawaii.

1 A: This book was written in 1955.
   B: You're wrong. It wasn't written in 1955.
   A: Really? When was it written?

2 A: The house is being redecorated next week.
   B: You're wrong. ....
   A: Really? When ....

3 A: Our new carpet will be delivered on Monday.
   B: You're wrong. ....
   A: Really? When ....

4 A: The meeting is going to be held on Friday.
   B: You're wrong. ....
   A: Really? When ....

5 A: The tourists have been taken to the museum.
   B: You're wrong. ....
   A: Really? Where ....

4 Rewrite the sentences in the *passive voice*.

1 Millions of people use the Internet every day.
   The Internet is used by millions of people every day.

2 Mrs Richards will mark your tests.
   ....

3 A neighbour had reported the murder.
   ....

4 An old lady saw the thief.
   ....

5 Mr Jones locks the office every evening.
   ....

6 Scientists have discovered a new species of dinosaur.
   ....

7 Isabella will write the article for next week's issue.
   ....

8 The ancient Greeks built the Parthenon.

5 Rewrite the sentences in the *passive voice*.

1 Anyone can answer this question.
   This question can be answered by anyone.

2 An old man was following the girls.
   ....

3 Detective Roberts is interviewing the robbers.
   ....

4 Jean Pierre is going to design her wedding dress.
   ....

5 A vet was examining the sick cat.
   ....

6 A doctor should treat that wound.
   ....

7 The new reporter can write that article.
   ....

8 Kate Woods might sing this song.
   ....

6 Say if these sentences are *active* (A) or *passive* (P). Then rewrite each sentence in the *active* or *passive voice*.

1 Someone is watching us.   A
   We are being watched.

2 Horror films shouldn't be watched by children.   P
   Children shouldn't watch horror films.

3 She is being examined by Doctor Simms.   ....

4 An old man found her purse.   ....

5 'Romeo and Juliet' was written by Shakespeare.   ....

6 This river has been polluted by poisonous chemicals.   ....

7 She was assisted by two young men.   ....

8 The prime minister will make an announcement.   ....

7 Rewrite the sentences in the *passive voice*. Include the agent only where necessary.

1 They are restoring the Leaning Tower of Pisa.
<u>The Leaning Tower of Pisa is being restored.</u>

2 Steven Spielberg directed these films.
....

3 Someone was following me on my way home.
....
....

4 The police haven't questioned the suspects yet.
....
....

5 Mr Newton is teaching the Geography class at the moment.
....
....

6 He told the students to keep quiet.
....
....

7 They invited a hundred people to the wedding.
....
....

8 Charlotte Brontë wrote 'Jane Eyre'.
....
....

8 Complete with *by* or *with*.

1 This picture was painted ......<u>by</u>...... a famous British artist.

2 These pictures were taken .... a very good camera.

3 My notes were blown away .... the wind.

4 He got stung .... a bee.

5 The room was filled .... smoke.

6 These pictures were taken .... a professional photographer.

7 Her desk was covered .... books.

8 The Statue of Liberty was designed .... F. Bartholdi.

B Make and let

See how these verbs form the passive voice.

Active voice	Passive voice
make somebody do something	be made to do something
My parents **make me tidy** my room every weekend.	**I am made to tidy** my room every my weekend.
let somebody do something	be allowed to do something
They **let me stay** up late.	**I am allowed to stay** up late.

9 Rewrite the sentences in the *passive voice*.

1 Our teachers make us work hard at school.
We <u>are made to work hard at school.</u>

2 She lets the children pick fruit from her trees.
The children ....

3 He made the boy apologise.
The boy ....

4 They don't let people touch the exhibits in the museum.
People ....

5 Mother will make you wear that dress!
You ....

6 The teacher will let us leave school early today.
We ....

7 She has never made me do anything like that!
....

8 They let us use the equipment.
....

C Double object verbs

There are some verbs that can have two objects (e.g. **give**, **send**, **bring**, **show**, **offer** etc.).
These verbs (**double object verbs**) form the **passive voice** in two ways, ie. we can form two different sentences with the same meaning.
Active voice: **They sent Tom a letter.**
Passive voice: **A letter was sent to Tom.**
Passive voice: **Tom was sent a letter.**

10 Rewrite the sentences in the *passive voice*.

1 The prime minister will give a medal to the winners.
A medal <u>will be given to the winners by the prime minister.</u>

2 He gave Tim some money.
Tim ....

3 They've offered Sally a job.
Sally ....

4 She is telling the children a story.
The children ....

5 They gave Bob a CD player for his birthday.
Bob ....

6 He must give the message to the right person.
The message ....

7 We teach our students English and French.
Our students ....

8 Someone brought flowers for the bride.
Flowers ....

9 They showed the tourists the sights of Athens.
The tourists ....

10 They pay her an excellent salary.
She ....

11 Rewrite the sentences using the word given.

USE OF FCE ENGLISH

1 They paid the artist £1,000 for this painting. **to**
£1,000 ....<u>was paid to</u>....... the artist for this painting.

2 They sent a brochure to all the members of the club. **been**
All the members of the club .... a brochure.

3 Someone delivered an important message to Mr Wilson this morning. **was**
An important message .... this morning.

4 She will offer tea and cakes to her guests. **be**
Her guests .... tea and cakes.

5 He showed the new computer room to the students. **was**
The new computer room .... the students.

D It is said that ... / He is said (to be)

Some verbs such as say, think, believe, expect, estimate, know, understand, report etc. form the passive voice in two ways:

- it + passive verb (+ that) + clause
- subject + passive verb + infinitive

Active: **Many people think (that) her new film is excellent.**
Passive: **It is thought (that) her new film is excellent.**
Her new film is thought to be excellent.

Active: **They say (that) he has won the lottery.**
Passive: **It is said (that) he has won the lottery.**
He is said to have won the lottery.

Active: **Some people believe (that) Mary left the country years ago.**
Passive: **It is believed (that) Mary left the country years ago.**
Mary is believed to have left the country years ago.

12 Rewrite the sentences in the *passive voice*. Use the correct construction.

1 It is said that a black cat brings bad luck.
A black cat is said <u>to bring bad luck.</u>

2 It is known that dogs are colour blind.
Dogs are known ....

3 It is believed that he has moved to Brazil.
He is believed ....

4 The thieves are reported to have escaped.
It is reported ....

5 It is said that five people died in the accident yesterday.
Five people are said ....

6 The plane is reported to have landed safely last night.
It is reported ....

7 The new restaurant is thought to be very good.
It is thought ....

8 The actor is said to be seriously ill.
It is said ....

9 It is thought that people came here three thousand years ago.
People ....

10 She is believed to have bought the painting for over a million pounds.
It is believed ....

13 Rewrite the sentences in the *passive voice*.
Use two constructions for each sentence.

1 They say that he's the richest man in Britain.
It is said that he's the richest man in Britain.
He is said to be the richest man in Britain.

2 They believe that she stole the jewellery.

....

....

3 People say that he has written a book about
ancient Greece.

....

....

4 Everyone knows that this is the oldest
building in town.

....

....

5 People say that she was a genius.

....

....

6 They say that he robbed a bank when he was
young.

....

....

7 They believe that she has discovered the
secret.

....

....

8 People say that dolphins are very intelligent.

....

....

14 Read and circle the correct answer.

STATUS: ENDANGERED

The Giant Panda

One of the world's largest mammals, the
giant panda, (1) .*b*.. to be one of the most
critically endangered species in the world.
Giant pandas (2) ..... be found in only six
small areas of central China. (3) It .....
estimated that there are fewer than 1000
pandas left in the wild.

Endangered? Why?

The giant panda (which is also (4) ..... as the
panda bear or bamboo bear) is being
threatened because the bamboo forests,
where it lives, (5) ..... destroyed. For years,
pandas (6) ..... illegally and unfortunately,
some are still being killed.

What is being (7) .....?

Recently, a very strict set of laws (8) .....
introduced (9) ..... the Chinese government
in order to protect these beautiful animals.
The protection of the giant panda is (10) .....
by many environmental organisations
around the world.

1 a is thinking	ⓑ is thought	c thinks	d thought
2 a can	b have	c are	d do
3 a is	b has	c is being	d had
4 a know	b knew	c known	d knowing
5 a have	b are	c must	d are being
6 a have hunted	b have been hunted	c have been hunting	d been hunted
7 a do	b doing	c did	d done
8 a did	b was	c has	d had
9 a by	b with	c from	d for
10 a support	b supported	c supporting	d supports

15 Rewrite the sentences using the word given.

1 Thousands of people attended the concert. **by**
   The concert ....was attended by........ thousands of people.

2 You must read this paragraph carefully. **read**
   This paragraph .... carefully.

3 They're going to restore that old building next month. **restored**
   That old building .... next month.

4 They didn't pay me last month. **get**
   I .... last month.

5 They will give £500 to the winner. **given**
   The winner .... £500.

6 The storm caused a lot of damage. **was**
   A lot of damage .... the storm.

7 They are cleaning the garage at the moment. **is**
   The garage .... at the moment.

8 They will not let you into the building. **be**
   You .... into the building.

9 His colleagues are organising a surprise party. **being**
   A surprise party .... his colleagues.

10 A ball broke the window. **by**
   The window .... a ball.

11 We should tell her about the party. **be**
   She .... about the party.

12 They were fixing the roof when I left. **was**
   The roof .... when I left.

16 Rewrite the sentences using the word given.

1 People think that this jewellery was made in Mexico. **thought**
   It .....is thought that..... this jewellery was made in Mexico.

2 It is expected that they will win the game. **are**
   They .... the game.

3 He offered her a rose. **was**
   She .... a rose.

4 It is said that this play was written in the seventeenth century. **have**
   This play .... written in the seventeenth century.

5 We don't know how many people were injured in the accident. **known**
   It .... how many people were injured in the accident.

6 This report must be sent to Mr Allan immediately. **sent**
   Mr Allan .... this report immediately.

7 It is reported that the missing girl was found in the park. **to**
   The missing girl is .... in the park.

8 They gave her a new sports car for Christmas. **given**
   She .... a new sports car for Christmas.

9 The bus driver is believed to have caused the accident. **is**
   It .... the bus driver caused the accident.

10 She told the students a joke. **were**
   The students .... a joke.

11 She is said to be very good at painting. **said**
   It .... very good at painting.

12 George Newton might be given a Nobel prize. **to**
   A Nobel prize .... George Newton.

17 Rewrite the numbered sentences in the *passive voice.*

STATUS: ENDANGERED

The Siberian Tiger

Like many other wild creatures, the largest member of the cat family – the Siberian tiger – is one of the most endangered species on Earth. (1) One <u>can find</u> Siberian tigers in eastern Siberia, Korea and China. (2) However, people <u>estimate</u> that only 150–200 tigers still exist in the wild. And there are about 250 tigers in zoos.

Endangered? Why?

(3) Experts <u>say</u> that human beings are the only enemy of the Siberian tiger. (4) In the twentieth century, hunters <u>reduced</u> the number of tigers in the wild by 95%. (5) Hunting <u>is still threatening</u> the Siberian tiger. (6) In China, they <u>use</u> tiger body parts for traditional medicine.

(7) What <u>can we do</u>?

(8) The Russian government <u>is making</u> efforts to protect the Siberian tiger. (9) In 1992, they <u>gave</u> it legal protection, through special laws against hunting. There are also many protected tiger areas in Siberia. However, according to experts, the Siberian tiger will soon become extinct, (10) unless we <u>take</u> more steps for its protection.

Like many other wild creatures, the largest member of the cat family – the Siberian tiger – is one of the most endangered species on Earth. Siberian tigers can be found in eastern Siberia, Korea and China. ....

....

....

....

....

....

....

Writing practice) Now you can do the **writing activity** for **Unit 9** (Teacher's Resource File).

Causative form

Grammar reference

A Form

	Active	Causative form
Present simple	We **clean** the windows.	We **have** the windows **cleaned**.
Present continuous	We **are cleaning** the windows.	We **are having** the windows **cleaned**.
Past simple	We **cleaned** the windows.	We **had** the windows **cleaned**.
Past continuous	We **were cleaning** the windows.	We **were having** the windows **cleaned**.
Present perfect simple	We **have cleaned** the windows.	We **have had** the windows **cleaned**.
Present perfect continuous	We **have been cleaning** the windows.	We **have been having** the windows **cleaned**.
Past perfect simple	We **had cleaned** the windows.	We **had had** the windows **cleaned**.
Past perfect continuous	We **had been cleaning** the windows.	We **had been having** the windows **cleaned**.
will	We **will clean** the windows.	We **will have** the windows **cleaned**.
going to	We **are going to clean** the windows.	We **are going to have** the windows **cleaned**.
Future continuous	We **will be cleaning** the windows.	We **will be having** the windows **cleaned**.
Future perfect simple	We **will have cleaned** the windows.	We **will have had** the windows **cleaned**.
Modal verbs	We **must clean** the windows.	We **must have** the windows **cleaned**.
Imperative	**Clean** the windows.	**Have** the windows **cleaned**.

> ▶ To form the **causative form**, we use:
> **have + object + past participle**
> **Active:**   The hairdresser cuts my hair once a month.
> **Causative:**   I have my hair cut once a month.
> ▶ Questions and the negative in the **present simple** and the **past simple** are formed
> using **do/does** and **did**.
> **We have our house painted every five years.**
> **We don't have our house painted every five years.**
> **How often do you have your house painted?**
> ▶ When we want to refer to who is doing the action, we use the **agent**, ie. **by +**
> **name/noun/pronoun.**
> **The Lombards had their house designed by a famous architect.**
> ▶ AInstead of **have**, we can use the verb **get**, mainly in oral speech.
> **You should get that suit cleaned.**

B   **Use**
> ▶ We use the **causative form** to refer to an action that we ourselves are not doing
> but have entrusted somebody else to do for us.
> Let's compare the following two examples.
> **Stephen repaired his car yesterday.** (He fixed it himself.)
> **Stephen had his car repaired yesterday by the mechanic.** (He did not fix it
> himself. The car mechanic fixed it.)
> ▶ We often use the **causative form** to talk about something unpleasant that
> happened to somebody.
> **Georgia had her handbag stolen last night.**

Grammar practice

1 Complete with the *causative form*. Use the tense given.

1   I _have my car washed_ (my car / wash) once a week. (present simple)

2   Jill .... (her house / break into) while she was in Spain. (past simple)

3   We .... (our living room/ redecorate). (present perfect)

4   Walter .... (the tap / fix) when I called him. (past continuous)

5   Don't worry. I .... (this film / develop) tomorrow. (will)

6   Mike's over there. He .... (his photograph / take). (present continuous)

7   I .... (this report / type) by Monday morning. (future perfect)

8   We .... (all our suitcases / send) to the hotel. (past simple)

9   Wanda .... (her hair / cut). (present continuous)

10 She .... (the article / translate). (past perfect)

2 Complete with the *causative form*.

1   We _are having our garage rebuilt_ (our garage / rebuild) at the moment.

2   Dad .... (his newspaper / deliver) to our house every morning.

3   She usually .... (her breakfast / serve) in her room.

4   He .... (his last book / publish) in 1999.

5   I .... (the letters / just / type).

6   The actor .... (his portrait / paint) two times so far.

7   The house .... (its roof / blow off) in the storm last night.

8   Sue .... (her carpets / clean) when I phoned.

9   They .... (the swimming pool / already / clean) when we visited them.

10 I .... (the door / fix) soon, I promise.

75

3 Form the negative and the question.

1. A: He had his bike fixed on Monday.
   B: You're wrong. <u>He didn't have it fixed on Monday.</u>
   A: Really? When <u>did he have it fixed?</u>

2. A: Bob had his briefcase stolen yesterday.
   B: You're wrong. ....
   A: Really? When ....

3. A: They've had air conditioning installed in the living room.
   B: You're wrong. ....
   A: Really? Where ....

4. A: She has her car serviced once a year.
   B: You're wrong. ....
   A: Really? How often ....

5. A: She will have her wedding dress made in Paris.
   B: You're wrong. ....
   A: Really? Where ....

6. A: We had the grass cut on Tuesday.
   B: You're wrong. ....
   A: Really? When ....

7. A: We're having our swimming pool cleaned tomorrow.
   B: You're wrong. ....
   A: Really? When ....

8. A: They're going to have their furniture replaced next week.
   B: You're wrong. ....
   A: Really? When ....

4 Rewrite the sentences using the *causative form*. Include the agent only where necessary.

1. A professional photographer took his picture.
   He <u>had his picture taken by a professional photographer.</u>

2. Someone stole Kate's bike this morning.
   Kate ....

3. The florist is going to deliver the flowers to my house at 9.30.
   I ....

4. A technician has just set up their new computer network.
   They ....

5. A secretary types Mr Evans' letters for him.
   Mr Evans ....

6. The children are washing Lisa's car for her.
   Lisa ....

7. A piano tuner tunes my piano once a year.
   I ....

8. The cleaner was vacuuming Bella's office when I called her.
   Bella ....

9. Fred's assistant will organise the meeting for him.
   Fred ....

10. Someone cooks her meals for her.
    She ....

5 Rewrite the sentences using the *causative form*.

1. We should ask someone to fix that hole in the wall.
   <u>We should have that hole in the wall fixed.</u>

2. I must ask someone to post this letter immediately.
   ....

3. Ask someone to photocopy this book, please.
   ....

4. You should ask your hairdresser to dye your hair red.
   ....

5. They have to clean our carpets this month.
   ....

6. The expert hasn't restored their painting yet.
   ....

7. The doctor should take his blood pressure.
   ....

8. Ask someone to clean the garage tomorrow.
   ....

9. I'll ask someone to serve our dinner before eight.
   ....

10. We are going to ask someone to repair the CD player.
    ....

6 Rewrite the sentences using the word given.

1 Diane always asks Jean Matie to make her clothes. **has**
Diane always _has her clothes made_ by Jean Matie.

2 Does someone clean your house every week? **have**
Do you .... every week?

3 We must ask the travel agent to make the arrangements for us. **have**
We must .... by the travel agent.

4 I have to ask someone to develop these photographs by tomorrow. **get**
I have to .... by tomorrow.

5 The watchmaker hasn't repaired my watch yet. **had**
I .... repaired yet.

6 Alexandra Jones is decorating Roy's office. **having**
Roy .... by Alexandra Jones.

7 You should ask someone to do this as soon as possible. **get**
You .... as soon as possible.

8 Has a dentist checked your teeth yet? **had**
Have you .... yet?

9 I wish the hairdresser hadn't cut my hair so short. **had**
I wish I .... my hair cut so short.

10 We must ask someone to make these copies at once. **have**
We must .... at once.

7 Read and complete. Use the *causative form*.

What's new in HOLLYWOOD?

by Darrin Sharpe

MARGARET ROSE, STAR OF STAGE AND SCREEN

Margaret Rose, star of stage and screen, is throwing a party to celebrate her new film. It will be held at Ms Rose's mansion on Sunday 14th March. For the last three months, Ms Rose (1) _has been having her home prepared_ (her home / prepare) by professionals. A week ago, she (2) .... (her mansion / redecorate) especially for the party. She also (3) .... (palm trees / plant) all around her garden. She (4) .... (a new swimming pool / just / build) as well! 'The old one was too small for all my guests,' she explained.

Ms Rose (5) .... (the food for the party / going to / cook) by French chefs. The dress that she will be wearing was designed two weeks ago. She (6) .... (it / make) by her good friend, designer Deborah Wayne. During the party, Ms Rose (7) .... (photographs / take) by fashion photographer Simon Richards.

She (8) .... (the invitations for the party / not send out) yet, but we do know that she (9) .... (1,500 invitations / already / print)!

Read all about the party in our next issue!

Oral practice Now you can do the **oral activity** for **Unit 10** (Teacher's Resource File).

Adjectives, adverbs

Teen Link

The Animal Files: Insect Facts

by Asta Brookes

Did you know that insects are **the most successful** life form on Earth? In fact, there are **more than** one million species of insects – almost 95% of all the animal species on Earth!

Insects have adapted **more successfully** to **different** climates **than** any other kind of animal. They can live in the air, on land, under the soil and in the water. The only place where they are not **commonly** found is the ocean.

Bees and butterflies are some of the **most useful** insects on Earth. By carrying pollen from one plant to the other, they help plants reproduce.

Grammar reference

A   Adjectives

▶ Adjectives are words that we use to describe a noun.
They go before the noun that they are describing or after verbs such as **be, look, sound, feel, smell, appear** etc.
We've bought a new car.
You look beautiful today.

▶ We can use more than one adjective to qualify a noun.
In this case, we use them in the following order, according to what they are expressing.

a/an	opinion	size	age	shape	colour	origin	material	purpose	noun
a		big		round			wooden	kitchen	table
a	fantastic		new		brown		leather		jacket
a	beautiful		old			Chinese			vase

▶ Some adjectives are used as nouns and refer to specific groups of people. We use **the** before these and they are followed by a plural verb. Some of them are:
We're organising a concert to raise money for the poor.
The young don't always understand the old.

B

Adverbs

Adverbs are words that usually qualify the verb in a sentence.

Formation of adverbs

▶ Some adjectives form adverbs by adding the ending **-ly**
(see Spelling rules, page 153.)
bad – badly
easy – easily
comfortable – comfortably
active – actively
beautiful – beautifully
logical – logically

▶ Some adverbs are not formed according to the rule, while some others take the same form as the adjective.

good – well	**early – early**
fast – fast	**near – near**
hard – hard	**high – high**
late – late	

▶ Some adjectives, eg. **hard, late, near, high,** form two adverbs with a different meaning.
- **hard** (hard), **hardly** (very little, almost not at all)
He works hard.
She's not my friend. We hardly know each other.
The phrase **hardly ever** means 'almost never'
He's always busy. He hardly ever goes out.
- **late** (late), **lately** (recently)
They got up late yesterday.
She's been working hard lately.
- **near** (close), **nearly** (almost)
There's a new bank quite near.
It's nearly ten o'clock.
- **high** (high), **highly** (very much, to a large extent)
The eagle flew high in the sky.
She is a highly intelligent girl.

Adverbs of manner

Adverbs of manner, **e.g.** well, badly, quietly **describe how something is done.**
He drives carefully.
It was raining heavily.

Adverbs of time

Adverbs of time, **e.g.** now, then, today, tomorrow, yesterday, indicate time.
I'll be back soon.
We saw him yesterday.

Adverbs of place

Adverbs of place, **e.g.** here, there, upstairs, nearby, indicate place.
They live nearby.

Adverbs of frequency

Adverbs of frequency, eg. **always, usually, often, frequently, sometimes, occasionally, rarely, seldom, never,** indicate the frequency with which something happens. They go:

- before the main verb.
We often visit our grandparents on Sundays.
- after an auxiliary verb.
They don't usually phone us so early in the mornings.
- after the verb **to be** when this is the main verb.
You're always late!

Modifying adverbs

▶ Modifying adverbs, eg. **very** (very), **quite** (quite), **rather** (a little), **fairly** (fairly), **really** (really), **almost** (almost), **extremely** (very much), **incredibly** (unbelievably) are used before the adjective or before any other adverb.
It's incredibly cold this morning.
The students are working quite hard this term.

▶ They are used to show the degree to which somebody or something has a characteristic.
My brother is rather shy, so he doesn't like going to parties.

▶ They are also used before a verb.
In this case, they go:
- before a main verb.
I absolutely love pancakes!
- after an auxiliary verb.
She didn't really like the film.

Position and order of adverbs

▶ Adverbs of manner usually go after the verb or after the object of a sentence.
He dressed quickly and left.
She did her homework quickly.

▶ Adverbs of place usually go after the verb or after the object of a sentence.
My friend and I meet here every day.

▶ Adverbs of time usually go at the end of the sentence. They can also go at the beginning.
Tomorrow we're having a party.
We're having a party tomorrow.

▶ When there is more than one adverb or adverbial phrases in a sentence, then we use them in the following order:
manner – place – time.
He's been working hard at school recently.

▶ But when there is a verb that indicates motion in the sentence, eg. **go, leave, come,** then we use the adverbs in the following order:
place – manner – time.
She arrived here early this morning.

11

Grammar practice

1 Put the adjectives in the correct order.

1 a(n) T-shirt – cotton, old, white   an old, white, cotton T-shirt
2 a necklace – silver, fantastic, new
3 a(n) scarf – silk, Chinese, expensive
4 hair – straight, short, dark
5 a frame – picture, wooden, square
6 a(n) car – modern, sports, Italian
7 a(n) chair – antique, French, valuable
8 a box – cardboard, big, black

2 Put the words in brackets in the correct place.

1 She speaks French. (fluently)
She speaks French fluently.

2 I'll be waiting for you. (tomorrow)

3 I've been here before. (never)

4 She felt tired this morning. (extremely)

5 Ray and Susan are married. (happily)

6 Wayne likes his job. (really)

7 We go out on Sundays. (hardly ever)

8 He drank his coffee. (quickly)

9 Maria is complaining about something. (always)

10 I've finished painting my room. (almost)

3 Put the words in the correct order.

1 I / went / yesterday / by bus / to work
I went to work by bus yesterday.

2 She / did / very quickly / last night / her homework

3 James / is / at this time of day / at school / usually

4 You / played / very well / last night / at the concert

5 He / has been working / all morning / hard / in his garden

6 We / meet / always / in the park / on Sunday mornings

7 She / waited / patiently / for hours / at the airport

8 I / get up / in the morning / usually / early

4 Circle the correct answer.

> **Tip**
>
> Adjectives qualify a noun.
> Adverbs usually indicate the manner, place, time, frequency or extent to which something happens.

1 He'll be very (angry) / angrily when he hears about this.

2 Don't be so rude / rudely to people!

3 It was dark and I couldn't see clear / clearly.

4 I usually feel very nervous / nervously before an exam.

5 We had a map, so we found the house easy / easily.

6 I might be a bit late / lately tonight.

7 Nick is a very careful / carefully driver.

8 I was so tired that I could hard / hardly keep my eyes open.

9 That test was really hard / hardly.

10 She sang beautiful / beautifully.

11 I'm not very good / well at Maths.

12 Have you been doing anything interesting late / lately ?

C Comparative and superlative forms

Adjectives

▶ We use the **comparative form** of adjectives to compare two people, animals or things with each other.
I think Physics is harder than Chemistry.
A small car is more economical than a big one.

▶ We use the superlative form of adjectives to compare more than two people, animals or things.
The tiger is the largest member of the cat family.
She is the best student in the class.

▶ Monosyllabic adjectives as well as disyllabic adjectives that end in –y form the comparative form with the ending –er and the word **than** after this (if the sentence continues). To form the superlative form, we add the article **the** before the adjective and the ending –est at the end of the adjective. (See Spelling rules, page 153)
hot – hotter –   the hottest
cheap – cheaper – the cheapest
pretty – prettier –   the prettiest

▶ Adjectives that have two or more syllables form the comparative form with the word **more** and the superlative form with the word **most** before the adjective.
modern – more modern – the most modern
difficult – more difficult – the most difficult

▶ Some disyllabic adjectives such as **clever, common, friendly, quiet, narrow, simple,** form the comparative and superlative form in both ways.
friendly – friendlier/more friendly –
the friendliest/the most friendly
simple – simpler/more simple –
the simplest/the most simple

Adverbs

▶ Adverbs ending in –**ly** form the comparative form with the word **more** and the superlative form with the word **most** before the adverb.
carefully – more carefully –
the most carefully

▶ Adverbs that have the same form as the adjective form the comparative form with the ending –er and the superlative form with the ending –est.
fast – faster – the fastest
hard – harder – the hardest

Irregular forms

▶ Some words do not form the comparative and superlative form according to the above rules.

Adjective/Adverb/Quantifier	Comparative	Superlative
good	better	the best
well	better	the best
bad	worse	the worst
badly	worse	the worst
far	farther/further	the farthest/furthest
old	older/elder	the oldest/eldest
(a) little	less	the least
much	more	the most
many	more	the most
a lot of/lots of	more	the most

D   Other forms of comparison

as ... as, not as/so ... as

▶ When we compare two people, animals or things that we want to show are the same, or do something in the same way, we use **as + adjective/adverb + as** (as ... as).
Janet's as old as Sue.

▶ To show that two people, animals or things are not the same or that they do not do something in the same way, we use **not as/so + adjective/adverb + as** (not as ... as).
He doesn't play the piano as well as his brother.

less + adjective/adverb (+ than)

▶ To show during a comparison that a person, animal or thing that we are comparing is inferior to the other, we can use **less + adjective/adverb (+ than)** (less ... than).
The first exercise was less difficult than the second one.

far/much/a lot/a little + comparative

▶ To express to what degree two people, animals or things differ, we can use the words **far/much/a lot** (a lot) or **a little** (a little) before the adjective or the adverb in the comparative form.

This book is much better than her previous one.
I got up a little later than usual this morning.

the + comparative, the + comparative

▶ This form has the meaning 'the more ..., the more ...'. Notice the word order in the sentence: ... **the + comparative + subject + verb, the + comparative + subject + verb.**
The sooner we leave, the sooner we'll get there.
The harder you study, the better you'll do at school.

comparative + and + comparative

▶ This form is used to express the meaning '...er and ...er'.
Your English is getting better and better.
He's growing taller and taller.

(It is) the + superlative + I've ever ...

▶ This form is used to express the meaning 'the most ... I have ever ...'.
That is the funniest story I've ever heard.

5   Complete the sentences with the correct form of the *adjectives* or *adverbs*.

The Animal Files:
Reptile Facts ▶

by Asta Brookes

* (1) <u>The fastest</u> (fast) reptile in the world is an iguana from Costa Rica.

* Most snakes can swallow animals that are (2) .... (wide) than their bodies.

* (3) .... (few) than 33% of the world's snake species are poisonous.

* (4) .... (large) species of frog in the world is the Goliath frog: it can grow as (5) .... (big) as an adult cat!

* A Colombian frog is (6) .... (poisonous) animal in the world. Its poison is (7) .... (dangerous) than that of a cobra.

* The world's (8) .... (old) turtle lived on the Galapagos Islands. It was 200 years old when it died! (9) .... (heavy) snake in the world was an anaconda.

* Snakes can hear as (10) .... (well) as people.

6 Rewrite the sentences using the word given.

1 My hair is long but yours is longer. **as**
My hair _isn't as long as_ yours.

2 Jack works harder than Tim. **not**
Tim .... as Jack.

3 David and Laura are both the same age.
old
David .... Laura.

4 Kate is very sensitive and her sister is equally sensitive. **as**
Kate .... her sister.

5 You don't know him as well as I do. **than**
I .... you.

6 Your bag weighs a lot but mine is heavier.
more
My bag .... yours.

7 My marks were bad but Jim's were worse.
so
My marks were .... Jim's.

8 This chair is comfortable and that one is, too. **as**
This chair .... that one.

9 Ben doesn't run as fast as Alex. **faster**
Alex .... Ben.

10 A car is safer than a motorbike. **so**
A motorbike .... a car.

11 The earrings are not as expensive as the ring. **is**
The ring .... the earrings.

12 Bettina did better than Kim in the exam.
as
Kim .... as Bettina in the exam.

7 Rewrite the sentences using *the + comparative, the + comparative.*

1 If you exercise more, you'll lose weight.
The more you exercise, the more weight you'll lose.

2 When you're young, you learn more easily.
....
....

3 If you practise more, you'll play better.
....
....

4 As we got closer to the airport, the noise became louder.
....
....

5 If you drive faster, we'll arrive there sooner.
....
....

6 If she eats a lot of sweets, she'll get fat.
....
....

7 If they try harder, their marks will be better.
....
....

8 If he waits any longer, the pain will get worse.
....
....

9 As she grew older, she became more difficult.
....
....

10 As they became richer, they became greedier.
....
....

11 When you get older, things become harder.
....
....

12 If he learns more about the subject, he will be more interested.
....
....

83

8 Compare the animals in the photos. Use different forms of comparison.

Shark   Dolphin   2   Elephant   Tiger

1

A dolphin isn't as dangerous as a shark.
A dolphin is more intelligent than a shark.
A shark can swim as well as a dolphin.

....
....
....

3 Monkey   Gorilla   4   Eagle   Parrot

....
....
....

9 Rewrite the sentences using the word given.

1   I've never heard such a good joke. **ever**
    It's the ......*best joke I've ever*...... heard.

2   He drives very carefully. **a**
    He's .... driver.

3   Her first novel wasn't as interesting as this one. **less**
    Her first novel .... this one.

4   I didn't like the film as much as Larry did. **than**
    Larry liked .... I did.

5   If you work harder, you'll earn more money. **the**
    The harder ....
    you'll earn.

6   I almost never watch television. **hardly**
    I .... television.

7   I've never read such a bad book. **the**
    This is ....
    ever read.

8   Becky is more beautiful than Sarah. **as**
    Sarah ....
    Becky.

9   If you get more sleep, you'll feel better.
    the
    The .... better
    you'll feel.

10 Their house cost more than ours. **as**
    Our house didn't ....
    theirs.

11 She plays tennis very well. **a**
    She ....
    tennis player.

12 If you are more careful, you'll make fewer mistakes. **the**
    The ....
    fewer mistakes you'll make.

10 Read and circle the correct answer.

TeenLink

The Animal Files:
Bird Facts ▶
by Asta Brookes

Our monthly 'Animal Files' feature is becoming (1) ..b... In fact, we received 100 bird facts from readers in (2) ..... a week! Anyway, this month we are focusing on birds. We're sure you'll find these amazing facts as interesting (3) ..... we did.

✷ Birds have (4) ..... eyesight than people. A hawk's eyes, for example, are eight times (5) ..... sharp as ours.

✷ The normal body temperature of a bird is usually 7–8 degrees (6) ..... ours. Their blood contains (7) ..... oxygen than human blood. A bird's heart beats (8) ..... more quickly than the human heart. When a bird rests, its heart can beat 400 times a minute. And when it flies, it beats even (9) ..... .

✷ The bones of a bird are usually (10) ..... flexible than ours. Birds can fly (11) ..... because their bones contain air, which makes their skeleton lighter.

1 a popular and popular   (b) more and more popular   c popular and more popular   d more popular than
2 a less from   b a little   c the least   d less than
3 a as   b so   c than   d from
4 a as good   b well   c better   d the best
5 a as   b more   c very   d almost
6 a more highly than   b as highly as   c higher than   d higher
7 a most   b a lot of   c much   d more
8 a most   b very   c far   d less
9 a the most rapidly   b more and more rapid   c more rapid   d more rapidly
10 a very   b less   c far   d the most
11 a easy   b easily   c much easier   d easier

Writing practice Now you can do the **writing activity** for **Unit 11** (Teacher's Resource File).

Infinitive, gerund

infinitive, 'let/make', 'would rather', 'had better',
'too/enough', gerund, 'be/get used to', 'prefer/would rather'

Grammar reference

A

Infinitive

The infinitive is the basic form of a verb. There are two forms of infinitive:

- full infinitive (infinitive with 'to') e.g. **to study**.
- bare infinitive (infinitive without 'to') e.g. **study**.

Full Infinitive
We use the full infinitive:
▶ after some verbs.

advise	choose	hate	mean	remember
afford	continue	help	offer	remind
agree	decide	hope	plan	seem
allow	deserve	intend	prefer	start
appear	expect	invite	prepare	stop
arrange	force	learn	pretend	try
ask	forget	like	promise	want
beg	go on	love	refuse	would like
begin	happen	manage	regret	would love

We've decided to move to Wales.
He promised to be more careful in the future.
I'd love to come with you.

▶ after some adjectives such as **anxious, glad, happy, lucky, pleased, prepared, ready, sorry, surprised, willing,** etc. in the syntax **subject + to be + adjective + infinitive.**
I'm very pleased to hear this.
She's always willing to help.

▶ with the syntax **it + to be + adjective.**
It is important to follow the teacher's instructions.

▶ In sentences with verbs like **want, expect, ask, would like,** etc. we can have a different subject, ie. the subject of the main verb may be different from the subject of the infinitive. In this case, the subject of the infinitive is usually a pronoun, a noun or a proper name and goes immediately after the main verb.

I want to post this letter.
(same subject)
I want you to post this letter.
(different subject)

We expected to win the match.
(same subject)
We expected the other team to win the match. (different subject)

Bare infinitive
We use the **bare infinitive:**

▶ after **modal verbs** such as **can, could, may, might, must, should,** etc.
You should see a doctor.

▶ after the verb **help.** But we can also use the **full infinitive.**
He helped me carry the books.
He helped me to carry the books.

B   let, make

The verbs **let** and **make** are followed by the **bare infinitive.**
Dad won't let me use his computer.
She always makes me laugh.

In the passive voice though, the verb **make** is followed by the **full infinitive.** The verb **let** is not used in the passive voice. Instead, we use the verb **allow**, which is followed by the **full infinitive.** (See also **Unit 9, The Passive, page 69**).

Active:	My parents make us eat plenty of fruit and vegetables.
Passive:	We are made to eat plenty of fruit and vegetables.
Active:	My parents will let me go to the party.
Passive:	I will be allowed to go to the party.

C   would rather, had better

▶ We use the **bare infinitive** after the expression **would rather** (= I would prefer).
I'd rather have a cup of tea.

▶ We use the **bare infinitive** after the expression **had better** (= should, it is a good idea to …)
You'd better clean up this mess before Mum gets back.

Grammar practice

I   Circle the correct answer.

1   You can ask Peter *drive* / (*to drive*) you to the station.

2   Let me *help* / *to help* you with that suitcase.

3   Hi! I'm so glad *see* / *to see* you!

4   You'd better *hurry* / *to hurry* or we'll be late.

5   Paul and Anne have decided *get* / *to get* married.

6   May I *use* / *to use* your phone?

7   That was close! You're lucky *be* / *to be* alive!

8   We can't afford *buy* / *to buy* a new car.

9   Could you *hold* / *to hold* this bag for me, please?

10 James has agreed *lend* / *to lend* us the money.

2 Complete with the *full infinitive* or *bare infinitive*.

We'd better tidy up the kitchen.

1 We'd better .... *tidy* .... (tidy) up the kitchen, or mother will be furious!

2 I'll never .... (speak) to him again!

3 I haven't been able .... (finish) that article.

4 You should .... (stay) in bed if you're not feeling well.

5 Students are not allowed .... (use) the library.

6 Why don't we .... (go) to a restaurant tonight?

7 I'd rather .... (wait) a bit longer if you don't mind.

8 It was great .... (hear) from you!

9 Mum made me .... (clean) my room this morning.

10 You ought .... (talk) to your boss about this.

11 We're going to the cinema. Would you like .... (join) us?

12 I'm really sorry .... (hear) that your mum isn't feeling well.

13 Do you think Ralph will let us .... (borrow) his car?

14 Are you willing .... (give up) your spare time to help us?

15 I'd better .... (tell) my parents I'll be home late tonight.

3 Rewrite the sentences using the word given.

1 My sister doesn't mind if I wear her clothes. **lets**
My sister .... *lets me wear* .... her clothes.

2 She wanted to be a teacher but her parents forced her to study medicine. **made**
She wanted to be a teacher but her parents ....
medicine.

3 Mum says I must drink a glass of orange juice every morning. **makes**
Mum .... a glass of orange juice every morning.

4 My parents don't allow me to go out alone after eight. **let**
My parents .... out alone after eight.

5 The robbers forced us to give them our money. **made**
The robbers ....
them our money.

6 Dad didn't allow me to use his car. **let**
Dad .... his car.

7 Our teacher wants us to work very hard. **makes**
Our teacher ....
very hard.

8 Do you think the boss will allow me to leave early today? **let**
Do you think the boss ....
.... early today?

9 Did she make them apologise to their teacher? **force**
Did .... to their teacher?

10 Why do you let him behave like that? **allow**
Why do you ....
like that?

4 Complete with *had better* or *would rather*.

1 We .....*had better*..... tell her the truth or she'll be very upset.

2 I don't want to stay at home. I .... come with you.

3 I don't like going by bus. I .... walk.

4 You don't look very well. You .... stay in bed today.

5 I .... stay at home. I don't really want to go to the cinema.

6 You .... study harder if you want to pass the exam.

7 .... you .... have tea or coffee?

8 We .... leave now or we'll miss the bus.

D too, enough

We can use the **infinitive** after the words **too** and **enough**.

▶ **too + adjective/adverb + infinitive**
The word **too** has a negative meaning and means 'too much, more than what it should or need be'.
I'm too short to reach the top shelf.

▶ **(not) adjective/adverb + enough + infinitive**
The word **enough** means 'enough' and has a positive meaning. We use it to say that something is (or is not) enough for something else to happen.
I'm not tall enough to reach the top shelf.

▶ **enough + noun + infinitive**
Enough is also used before a noun. But in this case, the word order is different.
Have we got enough money to buy the tickets?

▶ In the event that we have a different subject, ie. if the subject of the main verb is different to the subject of the infinitive, we have to add **for** and the new subject before the infinitive: **too + adjective/adverb + for somebody + infinitive**.
That shelf is too high. (Its subject is = That shelf.)
Toby can't reach it. (Its subject **can reach** = **Toby**).
That shelf is too high for Toby to reach.
NB: The subject of the main verb (**That shelf**) is also the object of the infinitive (**it**). We have to take the word **it** out of the sentence.

---

5 Rewrite the sentences using the word given.

1 She's too young to vote. (old)
She isn't old enough to vote.

2 He was driving too carelessly to avoid the accident. (carefully)
....

3 I'm not tall enough to reach that shelf. (short)
....

4 The students aren't interested enough to concentrate. (bored)
....

5 She's too shy to make a speech in public. (confident)
....

6 He didn't work fast enough to finish on time. (slowly)
....

7 Some people are too impatient to be good teachers. (patient)
....

8 We didn't get up early enough to catch the train. (late)
....

9 You didn't play well enough to beat her. (badly)
....

10 I felt too ill to go to school. (well)
....

11 The children are too young to watch that film. (old)
....

12 The actor doesn't look young enough to play the role. (old)
....

6 Read and complete with *too*/*enough* and the *infinitive*.

```
┌──────────────────────── untitled ────────────────────────┐
│  ✉                                                        │
│  ┌─────────────────────────────────────────────────────┐ │
│  │ From:     Heather Smith                              │ │
│  ├─────────────────────────────────────────────────────┤ │
│  │ To:       Liz Evans                                  │ │
│  ├─────────────────────────────────────────────────────┤ │
│  │ Subject:  Concert                                    │ │
│  └─────────────────────────────────────────────────────┘ │
```

Dear Liz,

I hope you are feeling better. Just stay in bed like the doctor said, and I'll see you soon.

Anyway, I went to the concert last night, after all. Let me tell you about it.

Justin called me at the last minute and said that he was (1) __too busy to come__ (busy / come) with me. I then called Zoe but she preferred to stay at home. She said she wasn't (2) .... (interested / make) the effort to come. I even asked my dad to come with me but he said he was (3) .... (old / go) to a pop concert. So in the end, I went by myself.

Anyway, I didn't really have a good time. It was freezing and I wasn't dressed (4) .... (warmly / feel) comfortable. I couldn't take any pictures at the concert, so I can't show you any. I had left my camera at home and by the time I realised, there wasn't (5) .... (time / go) back and get it. The music was great but I felt (6) .... (cold / relax) and I was also (7) .... (lonely / enjoy) myself.

I just wish you had been (8) .... (well / join) me. We would have had a great time together!

Love,
Heather

---

7 Join the sentences using the word given.

> ⎧ **Tip** ══════════════════════
> │ When the subject of the infinitive is different
> │ from the subject of the main verb, we usually
> │ use **for** and a pronoun, noun or proper
> │ name before the infinitive.
> │ **That jacket was too expensive for me to**
> │ **buy.**

1 The teacher's question was very difficult. Charles couldn't answer it. (too)
   The teacher's question was too difficult for Charles to answer.

2 The music wasn't loud. Iris couldn't hear it. (enough)
   ....

3 The problem was very complicated. Sean couldn't solve it. (too)
   ....

4 The blue sweater wasn't big. He couldn't wear it. (enough)
   ....

5 There wasn't much milk. She couldn't feed the cat. (enough)
   ....

6 The kitchen table was too heavy. Wayne couldn't move it by himself. (too)
   ....

7 It wasn't warm. We couldn't go to the beach. (enough)
   ....

8 It was very late. I couldn't call her. (too)
   ....

9 He spoke very softly. The audience couldn't hear him. (too)
   ....

10 There isn't much time. We can't go shopping today. (enough)
   ....

E Gerund

We form the **gerund** by adding the ending –ing to a verb. (See Spelling rules, page 152.)

We use the **gerund**:
▶ as a noun, either as the subject or as the object of a verb.
Learning English is easy.
▶ after some verbs.

admit	intend	prefer
avoid	keep	propose
begin	like	quit
continue	look forward	recommend
deny	to	regret
enjoy	love	remember
finish	mean	start
forget	mention	stop
go	mind	suggest
go on	miss	try
hate	practise	

He goes fishing on Sundays.
I avoid staying up late on weekdays.

▶ after the expressions **can't stand, can't help, feel like, it's no use, it's no good, it's not worth, there's no point (in), have difficulty (in).**
I feel like going out tonight.
It's not worth spending so much money on CDs.
▶ after prepositions
She left without saying goodbye.
You can open the bag by cutting along the dotted line.
They accused me of stealing the money.

be afraid of	be good at
be bad at	be guilty of
be bored with	be interested in
be crazy about	be keen on
be fed up with	be sorry for
be fond of	be tired of

▶ after some expressions that end in a preposition such as:
I'm not very good at playing tennis.
Are you really interested in ancient history?

---

8 Choose and complete with the correct form of the verb.

call	lie	paint	shop	try
clean	listen	play	steal	watch
go	open	see	travel	work

He's always been good at painting.

1 He's always been good at ......painting...... .
   Have you see his latest picture?

2 You should practise .... the piano more often.

3 He hasn't finished .... the living room yet. He still has to vacuum the carpet.

4 I always have a glass of milk before .... to bed.

5 I can't stand .... to that kind of music.

6 Are you accusing me of .... to you?

7 .... first class by plane is very expensive.

8 I don't feel like .... TV right now.

9 I hate .... late at the office.

10 Would you mind .... the window?

11 I'm going .... with Carol in the afternoon.

12 I look forward to .... you soon.

13 He admitted .... the money.

14 It's no use .... to fix that. It's broken.

15 There's no point .... her now.

F   be used to, get used to

▶ The expression used to means 'I am accustomed to doing something'. It is followed by a gerund.
We moved to this city many years ago, so I am used to living here.

▶ The expression get used to means 'get used to/become accustomed to doing something'. It is followed by a gerund.
We moved to this city a few weeks ago. It's different from our village but I am slowly getting used to living here.

▶ We can use the expressions be used to and get used to in different tenses or with modal verbs.

When we first moved here, I wasn't used to living in the city centre.

We moved here many years ago. Now I'm used to living in the city centre.

He must be used to living in the city centre. He's lived here all his life.

I still haven't got used to living in the city centre.

Don't worry. You'll soon get used to living in the city centre.

We're slowly getting used to living in the city centre.

I have to get used to living in the city centre.

▶ Be careful not to confuse the expression be used to with used to. Used to is used for a habit that somebody had in the past and is followed by the infinitive. Compare the examples.
I'm used to getting up early. (I am used to waking up early.)

I used to get up early. (I used to wake up early in the past, but not any more.)

9   Complete with the correct form of *be/get used to*.

1   I can't .....*get used to living*..... (live) in this noisy neighbourhood.

2   I'll just have a glass of milk, thank you. I .... (not / have) a big meal at this time of day.

3   I've been at this school for a month now but I still haven't .... (speak) English in the classroom.

4   When she first moved in with Sarah, she .... (not / share) a flat with someone else but she doesn't find it so hard now.

5   Don't worry. You will soon .... (ride) your new bike.

6   Everyone in my family is a vegetarian, so I .... (eat) vegetables every day.

7   Georgia is nervous. This is her first concert and she .... (not / sing) in front of so many people.

10 Read and circle the correct answer.

> **Tip**
>
> Be/get used to is followed by a gerund. Used to is followed by the infinitive.

Change of habit

Last week, Leslie Banks interviewed our new French teacher, Madame Bernard.

She came to Britain a year ago. She's had to change her habits and she's still trying to (1) *be / get* used to her new lifestyle. Madame Françoise Bernard, our new French teacher, told us a few things about her life in Britain.

'I still haven't got used to (2) *live / living* in the city centre. I used to (3) *live / living* in a small village in Brittany. Life is so different here!

Back in France, I (4) *used to / am used to* live with my parents. I (5) *am not used to / didn't use to* spending so much time by myself, so sometimes I get a bit lonely.

I don't live near the school and it takes me almost an hour to get to work. But this is not a problem. I am (6) *used to travelling / used to travel* long distances. I (7) *used to do / am used to doing* it every day in France. I have got a car but I take the bus to work. I haven't got used to (8) *drive / driving* on the left yet.

The thing I miss most of all is home cooking! My mother (9) *is used to doing / used to do* all the cooking at home, so I never had to learn how to do it myself. I'm not used to (10) *prepare / preparing* my own meals but now I don't have a choice. Thank goodness I am getting better.'

G

Infinitive and gerund

▶ Some verbs are either followed by the **infinitive** or by a **gerund**, without there being any important difference in the meaning. These verbs are: begin, continue, hate, intend, like, love, prefer, start.

The audience began cheering when the singer walked onto the stage.
The audience began to cheer when the singer walked onto the stage.

She prefers doing her homework in the evenings.
She prefers to do her homework in the evenings.

▶ Some verbs have a different meaning according to whether they are followed by the **infinitive** or by a **gerund**. These verbs are:

- stop

  stop + infinitive (stop doing something in order to do something else)
  I stopped to buy a comic on my way home. (I stopped to buy a comic.)

  stop + gerund (stop doing something)
  (I've stopped buying comics.)

- try

  try + infinitive (try to do something)
  I tried to get to sleep but I couldn't. (I tried to sleep but I couldn't.)

  try + gerund (try to do something)
  If you can't fall asleep, try drinking some warm milk before bedtime. (If you can't sleep, try (to drink) a glass of hot milk before going to bed.)

- **remember**

  remember + infinitive (remember to do something) **Did you remember to call her last night** (Did you remember to call her last night?)

  remember + gerund (Don't you remember calling her last night?) **Don't you remember calling her last night?** (Don't you remember calling her last night?)

- **forget**

  forget + infinitive (forget to do something) **I forgot to call him last night.** (I forgot to call him last night.)

  forget + gerund (forget, not remember something that I did in the past) **I'll never forget visiting London for the first time.** (I will never forget my first visit to London.)

- **regret**

  regret + infinitive (to regret something) **I regret to tell you that he has not accepted your offer.** (I regret to have to inform you that he has not accepted your offer.)

  regret + gerund (regret something that I did in the past) **He regrets not accepting the offer.** (He regrets not accepting the offer.)

- **go on**

  go on + infinitive (continue, carry on doing something) **She told us about her childhood. Then she went on to tell us about the things she did at university.** (She told us about her childhood. Then she told us what she did at university.)

  go on + gerund (continue to do something that I have already been doing) **He went on talking about his life in the USA.** (He continued to talk about his life in the USA.)

- **mean**

  mean + infinitive (mean to do something) **I'm sorry. I didn't mean to worry you.** (Sorry. I didn't mean to worry you.)

  mean + gerund (mean, presuppose) **I'll finish the article even if it means staying up late.** (I'll finish the article, even if it means I have to stay up late.)

- **need**

  The verb **need** may either be followed by the **infinitive** or by a **gerund**. When it is followed by a gerund, it has a passive meaning. **We need to paint the bedrooms.** **The bedrooms need painting.**

11 Complete with the *infinitive* or *gerund*.

1 The doctor advised her ....*to stay*.... (stay) in bed for a few days.

2 When do you intend .... (leave) for the USA?

3 I have to .... (practise) playing the piano more often.

4 I hate .... (have) to stay at home on a Saturday night.

5 Everyone started .... (laugh) when she dropped the cake.

6 Don't worry. I don't mind .... (wait).

7 Do you really think they deserved .... (win) the game?

8 We still haven't finished .... (redecorate) the house.

9 I can't afford .... (buy) a new computer right now.

10 She refused .... (tell) us what happened last night.

12 Rewrite the sentences.

1 We need to clean the windows.
The windows *need cleaning.* ....

2 Our bedroom needs painting.
We ....

3 You will need to wash your car.
Your car ....

4 His computer needed fixing.
Someone ....

5 Those letters need typing.
The secretary ....

6 You need to iron your shirt.
Your shirt ....

7 We needed to mop the floor.
The floor ....

8 The grass needs cutting.
She ....

13 Complete with the *infinitive* or *gerund*.

1 I regret ......*to tell*...... (tell) you that you have not passed your exam. I know you worked very hard.

2 Who told her about the party? I don't remember .... (say) anything about it last night.

3 I'm going to buy that car, even if it means .... (spend) all my money!

4 Don't forget .... (call) me as soon as you arrive.

5 He told the police how the accident had happened. Then he went on .... (say) that it wasn't his fault.

6 I'm sorry. I didn't mean .... (sound) so rude.

7 James is a vegetarian. He stopped .... (eat) meat years ago.

8 If you can't find him at home, try .... (call) him at the office.

9 I'll never forget .... (meet) my favourite film star.

10 I regret .... (lie) to him. I should have told him the truth.

11 We stopped .... (have) a cup of coffee on our way home. That's why we're late.

12 Did you remember .... (pay) the phone bill or will I have to do it tomorrow?

14 Rewrite the sentences.

1 Playing golf is fun.
It *'s fun to play golf.*

2 It's easy to learn how to drive.
Learning ....

3 It's difficult to learn Chinese.
Learning ....

4 Visiting the Louvre was exciting!
It ....

5 It will be very hard to pass this exam.
Passing ....

6 It's nice to be able to help people.
Being ....

7 Playing with matches is dangerous.
It ....

8 It's illegal to park here.
Parking ....

9 Travelling to Hawaii would be wonderful!
It ....

10 Working in a factory won't be easy.
It ....

15 Read and complete with the *infinitive* or *gerund*.

It was my sister's birthday and we had arranged (1) ......*to have*.... (have) dinner at a Chinese restaurant that night. It was 8.30 and I was almost ready (2) .... (leave). I had just finished (3) .... (put) on my make-up when I realised that I hadn't bought her a present!

It was too late (4) .... (buy) anything and I knew that she would never forgive me for (5) .... (forget) her birthday.

I had (6) .... (do) something. Then I had an idea. I decided (7) .... (give) her a book which I had had for about a year but which I had never read. I took it out of my bookcase, wrapped it quickly and left for the restaurant.

Tina was really happy (8) .... (see) that I had got her a present. She thanked me for (9) .... (be) so thoughtful. But she had a strange expression on her face when she unwrapped it. 'Do you really expect me (10) .... (believe) that you bought this for me?' she said. 'I gave you this book for your birthday ten months ago!'

I prefer, would rather

▶ We use **prefer** with the following types of syntax to say what we generally prefer.

prefer + gerund/noun (+ to + gerund/noun)	I prefer reading. I prefer reading to watching television. They prefer vanilla ice cream. They prefer vanilla ice cream to chocolate ice cream.
prefer + full infinitive (+ rather than + bare infinitive)	I prefer to read. I prefer to read rather than watch television.

▶ We use **prefer** to say what we would prefer to do in a specific case.

would prefer + full infinitive (+ rather than + bare infinitive)	I would prefer to stay at home tonight. I would prefer to stay at home rather than go out tonight.

▶ We usually use **would rather** to say what we would prefer to do in a specific case. **Would rather** is followed by the **bare infinitive** and is usually used with the following syntax:

would rather + bare infinitive (+ than + bare infinitive)	I would rather stay at home. I would rather stay at home than go to the cinema tonight.

▶ In a case where we have a different subject, ie. if the subject of the main verb is different from the subject of the infinitive, notice how **prefer** and **would rather** are formed.

	Same subject	Different subject
prefer	(would) prefer to do sth I (would) prefer <u>to water</u> the garden before dinner.	(would) prefer sb to do sth I (would) prefer <u>you to water</u> the garden before dinner.
would rather	would rather do sth I would rather <u>water</u> the garden before dinner.	would rather + somebody + past simple I would rather <u>you watered</u> the garden before dinner.

16 Complete with the *full infinitive, bare infinitive* or *gerund*.

1 I would prefer ....*to stay*.... (stay) a bit longer.

2 She prefers .... (go) shopping on Saturdays.

3 I would rather .... (call) him after lunch.

4 They prefer .... (drink) a cup of hot tea in the evenings.

5 I would prefer .... (think) about this for a few days.

6 Would you rather .... (go) by train?

7 We prefer .... (have) dinner early in the evenings.

8 I would rather .... (spend) the weekend with my grandparents.

17 Complete with the *full infinitive, bare infinitive* or *gerund.*

1 I'd rather ......*buy*...... (buy) a new dress for the party than ......*wear*...... (wear) this one.

2 I prefer .... (go) to a restaurant to .... (eat) at home.

3 I'd rather .... (leave) now than .... (wait) for Chris.

4 I'd prefer .... (work) harder rather than .... (borrow) the money.

5 I prefer .... (drive) to .... (travel) by train.

6 I'd rather .... (sit) in the garden than .... (stay) in my room all day.

7 I'd prefer .... (finish) this now rather than .... (work) in the evening.

8 In my free time, I prefer .... (listen) to music rather than .... (play) video games.

18 Rewrite the sentences.

1 I would rather take a taxi than go by bus.
I would prefer *to take a taxi rather than go by bus.*

2 I would prefer to listen rather than talk.
I would rather ....

3 I would prefer to watch a film on TV rather than go to the cinema.
I would rather ....

4 I would rather have some tea than drink more coffee.
I would prefer ....

5 I would prefer to think about the problem rather than answer right now.
I would rather ....

6 I would rather cook than wash the dishes.
I would prefer ....

7 I would rather redecorate my flat than move to a new one.
I would prefer ....

8 I would rather read a good book than watch TV.
I would prefer ....

19 Complete with the correct form of the verb.

1 Please don't tell her about the accident. I'd rather she ..*didn't know*.. (not know).

2 I'd rather .... (sit) over there.

3 I'd rather you .... (not read) this letter.

4 Would you rather I .... (do) the shopping today?

5 Would you rather .... (have) dinner at home or go to a restaurant?

6 I'd rather we .... (talk) about this later.

7 I would rather .... (finish) my homework before going out.

8 I'd rather .... (not tell) her I failed. She'll be very disappointed.

20 Rewrite the sentences using the word given.

1 I'd rather fix this computer than buy a new one. **than**
I'd prefer to fix this computer ..*rather than buy*.. a new one.

2 Talking with your mouth full is not polite. **to**
It's .... with your mouth full.

3 The coffee was so hot that I couldn't drink it. **too**
The coffee was .... drink.

4 I try not to eat sweets. **avoid**
I .... sweets.

5 The police officer didn't let me park outside the hospital. **allow**
The police officer didn't .... outside the hospital.

6 I'd prefer to wait here rather than stand in the rain. **rather**
I'd .... in the rain.

7 He forced me to give him the money. **made**
He .... him the money.

Writing practice Now you can do the **writing activity** for **Unit 12** (Teacher's Resource File).

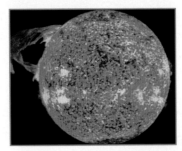

Nouns, articles

Teen Link

Trivial facts:
Did you know?

by John Parker

- **The herring (a kind of fish)** produces 50,000 **eggs a season**.
- **Bulls** (and **cows**) can only see in black and white.
- There are more than one million animal **species** in **the world**.
- **An iceberg** contains more **heat** than **a match**.
- **Aircraft** are not allowed to fly over **the Taj Mahal**.

- **The Sun** is about 330,000 **times** larger than **the Earth**.
- No **piece of paper** can be folded in half more than seven **times**.

Grammar reference

A	Nouns
	Countable nouns ▶ Nouns that can be counted using numbers and have a plural are called countable nouns.

Uncountable nouns

▶ Nouns that cannot be counted using numbers and that do not have a plural are called uncountable nouns. Uncountable nouns are usually:
* food: bread, butter, cheese, chocolate, coffee, flour, meat, salt, sugar etc.
* liquids: milk, oil, petrol, water etc.
* materials: aluminium, cotton, glass, gold, metal, nylon, paper, plastic, silk, silver, tin, wood, wool etc.
* nouns that express abstract ideas anger, democracy, freedom, hate, health, knowledge, love, luck etc.
* various others: advice, baggage, behaviour, damage, electricity, equipment, fun, furniture, hair (hair), help, homework, information, jewellery, luggage, money, news, rain, research, room (space), rubbish, sand, time (time), traffic, transport, weather, work etc.

▶ To refer to the quantity of uncountable nouns, we use measuring units, eg. a kilo, a litre, a gram, or some other expressions that can define it.

a bar of chocolate	a glass of water	a packet of tea
a bottle of milk	a gram of powder	a piece of cake
a bowl of rice	a jar of honey	a sachet of tea
a can of coke	a kilo of meat	a sack of flour
a carton of juice	a litre of water	a tin of soup
a cup of coffee	a loaf of bread	a tube of toothpaste

▶ Many of the above expressions may also be used with countable nouns: a packet of biscuits, a tin of peas, a kilo of potatoes.

▶ The expression a piece of is used with a lot of uncountable nouns.

a piece of advice	a piece of furniture	a piece of news
a piece of cheese	a piece of information	a piece of plastic
a piece of equipment	a piece of luggage	a piece of rubbish

▶ We can also use the expression a bit of/bits of.
a bit of information
a bit of bread
bits of paper

▶ Some nouns are used as countable and uncountable nouns but the meaning of the word changes.

Countable	Uncountable
a paper = newspaper, document	paper = paper
a hair = hair	hair = hair
a glass, glasses = glass, glasses	glass = glass
a room = room	room = space
an iron = iron (appliance)	iron = iron
(one) time = once	time = time

▶ There are other words that indicate quantity.
* The words some, any, no, a lot of and lots of can be used with countable and uncountable nouns.
* The words many and (a) few are only used with countable nouns.
* The words much and (a) little are only used with uncountable nouns.
Have you got any books on the subject?
I would like some advice.
I need to ask you a few questions.
There isn't much orange juice left.
We need a little more time.

Plural nouns

▶ Some nouns only have a plural and are followed by a plural verb. They usually refer to:
- things that consist of two parts, eg. **binoculars, glasses, jeans, pyjamas, scissors, shorts, sunglasses, tights, trousers** etc.
  These jeans are too tight.
- things that by their nature consist of a lot of similar units, pieces or parts, eg. **clothes, goods, stairs** etc.
  Your clothes are on the bed.

Singular and plural nouns

▶ There are some nouns that, even if they are in the singular, are usually followed by a plural verb since they refer to groups of people. A singular verb may also follow them, however this occurs more rarely. Some of these are: **company, crew, family, government, orchestra, police, staff, team** etc.
The government have/has introduced a new set of laws.

▶ Some nouns, if they also end in –s, are singular nouns and the verb that follows them is always in the singular. Some of these are: **athletics, billiards, economics, electronics, gymnastics, maths, measles, mumps, news, physics, politics** etc.
Maths is my favourite subject.

▶ Some nouns end in –s both in the singular and in the plural, eg. **means, species, series.**
The car is a means of transport.
They used many means to persuade him.

The African elephant is an endangered species.
Many species of birds live on the island.

I enjoyed this series; it was funny.
There are many series on TV.

▶ Some other nouns are the same either in the singular or in the plural, eg. **sheep, deer.**

Grammar practice

I Choose and complete with the correct form of the words.

bar	bowl	cup	gram	loaf
bottle	can	glass	jar	piece (x3)

1 Can I have a ....*glass*........ of water, please?

2 That .... of furniture cost her £650.

3 I've bought a .... of honey for the pancakes.

4 Let me give you a .... of advice.

5 Please get me two .... of cooking oil from the supermarket.

6 He can't be hungry! He ate a .... of popcorn an hour ago!

7 I went to the baker's and got two .... of bread.

8 I'd love a .... of that chocolate cake.

9 I've eaten two .... of chocolate today.

10 Can you get me a .... of coke from the fridge?

11 You will need 100 .... of margarine for the cake.

12 I'll make you a nice .... of hot tea.

2 Circle the correct answer.

1 Look at you! You need to brush your (hair) / hairs!

2 Mirrors are usually made of *a glass / glass*.

3 Spinach is good for you because it contains a lot of *iron / irons*.

4 I'll have *a glass / glass* of orange juice, thank you.

5 Is there *a room / room* for my coat in that suitcase?

6 I had left some very important *paper / papers* on my desk.

7 Have you ever wished you could travel through *time / times*?

8 They make these notebooks from *a recycled paper / recycled paper*.

9 The hotel was excellent. We stayed in *a room / room* on the sixth floor.

10 He can't see very well without his *glass / glasses*.

11 There are dog *hair / hairs* all over the sofa!

12 Don't forget to buy *a paper / paper* so we can see what's on at the cinema this weekend.

3 Say if the underlined words are singular (S) or plural (P). Then circle the correct answer.

Sheep are not the most intelligent of animals.

1 <u>Sheep</u> *is* / (*are*) not the most intelligent of animals. ....P......

2 I've always thought that <u>politics</u> *is / are* a boring subject. ....

3 The <u>police</u> *has / have* arrested one of the robbers. ....

4 Why *is / are* your <u>clothes</u> covered in mud? ....

5 There *is / are* almost 4,000 <u>species</u> of plants in Greece. ....

6 I didn't buy the <u>trousers</u> because *it was / they were* too expensive. ....

7 Tyrannosaurus rex *was / were* a <u>species</u> of dinosaur. ....

8 The most economical <u>means</u> of transport *is / are* the bicycle. ....

9 <u>Deer</u> *lives / live* in herds, don't they? ....

10 The <u>scissors</u> *is / are* in that drawer. ....

11 My favourite TV <u>series</u> *is / are* 'The Wild West'. ....

12 Your <u>shorts</u> *looks / look* really funny! ....

13 <u>Physics</u> *isn't / aren't* as difficult as I thought. ....

14 The good <u>news</u> *is / are* that it won't cost more than £50. ....

B   Articles

Indefinite article: a/an

▶ The indefinite article a/an is used with singular countable nouns or before adjectives that accompany a countable noun. We usually use a before nouns or adjectives that start with a consonant and an before nouns or adjectives that start with a vowel.

a book, a funny story, an exam, an easy question

▶ However, there are some nouns or adjectives that, even if they start with a vowel, take a and not an. This happens because when we pronounce them, the first sound is a consonant, not a vowel.

an umbrella, a uniform
an exciting film, a European country

▶ There are also some words that start with a consonant but when we pronounce them, the first sound is a vowel.
These words take an, not a.

a house, an hour
a hot day, an honest man
a member of Parliament, an MP

▶ We use a/an:
- when we are referring to something specific.
  She's looking for a job. (any job, not a specific one)
- after the verb to be, when we refer to somebody's profession or to a virtue that somebody has.
  Ms Harris used to be a teacher.
  James is an excellent swimmer.
- with the phrases once/twice a week, three times a day, 50 km an hour, £2 a kilo etc.
  I work ten hours a day.

Definite article: the

The definite article is used with countable and uncountable nouns.

We use the:
▶ to talk about something specific or unique.
  Where's the CD I gave you this morning? (the specific CD that I gave you)
  The sky is blue. (There is only one sky.)
▶ before names of oceans (the Pacific), seas (the Black Sea), rivers (the Nile), deserts (the Sahara desert) and mountain ranges (the Andes).
▶ before the names of some countries or states such as the United Kingdom, the United States of America, the Netherlands, the Bahamas, the Philippines, the Czech Republic.

▶ before names of cinemas or theatres (the National Theatre), hotels (the President Hotel), museums (the Natural History Museum), newspapers (the Sun), specific buildings or monuments (the Eiffel Tower) and ships (the Titanic).
▶ before the names of families (the Browns, the Smiths) or nationalities (the French, the Chinese).
▶ when we use adjectives as nouns to refer to groups of people (the homeless, the unemployed, the young).
▶ with musical instruments (the piano, the guitar).
▶ in the superlative form of adjectives and adverbs (the best student).
▶ with the expressions in the morning, in the afternoon and in the evening, but not with the expressions at night, midnight though.
▶ with the words airport, cinema, theatre, bank, station etc., when we refer to their main function or the services that they offer.
  Let's go to the cinema tonight. BUT
  There's a new cinema in West Street.

Zero article

We do not use an article:
▶ before proper names (Thomas, Mary, Ms Harris).
▶ before plural countable nouns or before uncountable nouns when we are generally referring to these.
  Roses are beautiful. (roses generally)
  The roses he gave me were beautiful. (the specific roses that he gave me)

  Life can be very strange sometimes. ((life generally)
  The life he led was hard. (the life of a specific person)

  Money makes the world go round. (money generally)
  He lent me the money for the tickets. (the specific money for the tickets)
▶ before the names of countries (Denmark, Italy), cities (Paris, Athens), continents (Africa, Asia), mountains (Mount Olympus), streets (West Street), parks (Richmond Park), squares (Trafalgar Square) and lakes (Lake Baikal).
▶ before the names of games (chess, Monopoly), sports (skiing, tennis), school subjects (Maths, History), meals (breakfast, lunch, dinner) and languages (English, French, and the English language).

> ▶ before the words **bed, home, work, hospital, prison, church, school, university, college,** when we refer to their main function or their basic purpose. Compare the examples below.
> **John's at school.** (He is at school as a pupil, he is a pupil.)
> **John's father waited for him outside the school.** (He waited for him outside the building, the school premises.)
>
> **Fiona is in hospital.** (She is in hospital as a patient.)
> **I went to the hospital to see Fiona.** (I went to the hospital as a visitor.)

> ▶ with the phrases **watch television** and **listen to music.**
> **Let's watch television.** BUT
> **Turn on the television.** (the television = the appliance)
>
> **I love listening to music in my free time.**
> ▶ when we refer to a species of animal generally.
> **Cheetahs are the fastest mammals in the world.**
> ▶ However, we can use the article the and a singular noun to refer to a species of animal generally.
> **The cheetah is the fastest mammal in the world.**

4 Complete with *a/an* or *the*.

1 She gave him ......*a*...... book for his birthday.

2 Have you read .... book I gave you last week?

3 There's .... man here to see you.

4 .... boy in that photo is my cousin.

5 He visits his grandparents once .... week.

6 Is there .... airport in Birmingham?

7 I have to be at .... airport at six.

8 That was .... most amazing story I've ever heard.

9 Ms Jackson is .... university professor.

10 How often do you go to .... dentist?

5 Complete with *the* if necessary.

Trivial facts:
Did you know?

by Rachel Graham

■ It takes 8.5 minutes for light to travel from (1) ...*the*... Sun to (2) .... Earth.

■ (3) .... longest river in (4) .... world is (5) .... Nile, which is in (6) .... Africa.

■ The game of (7) .... squash originated in (8) .... United Kingdom.

■ (9) .... largest city in (10) .... China is (11) .... Shanghai.

■ (12) .... Antarctica is (13) .... only continent in the world that has no native population.

■ (14) .... Britain was the first country to issue (15) .... postage stamps.

■ Of all the words in (16) .... English language, the word 'set' has (17) .... most definitions.

6 Circle the correct answer.

> **Tip**
>
> With nouns such as **hospital**, **school**, **university**, **church**, etc. we use the article when we are referring to their main function, their basic purpose.

1 I'll be at (home) / the home after half past two.

2 I was very tired, so I went straight to bed / the bed.

3 Anne works as a nurse at hospital / the hospital in the centre of town.

4 He had an accident and was taken to hospital / the hospital.

5 What time do you finish work / the work on Fridays?

6 Mum has gone to school / the school to talk to my teacher.

7 She's studying medicine at university / the university.

8 The reporter went to prison / the prison to interview one of the guards.

9 Put your new clothes out on bed / the bed and we'll look at them.

10 Joanna doesn't work; she's still at school / the school.

7 Complete with *the* if necessary.

1 He lives in ......—...... Main Street.

2 I'm picking Jill up from .... station this afternoon.

3 I'll be back at .... noon.

4 Is .... Mount Everest in .... Himalayas?

5 What time do you usually get up in .... morning?

6 I'll be at .... work until six.

7 Who was .... girl you were talking to a few minutes ago?

8 We were having .... dinner when he called.

9 Did you visit .... Louvre when you were in .... Paris?

10 We go to .... church every Sunday.

11 I can't remember .... Doctor Roberts' phone number.

12 I called .... doctor and he said I should stay in .... bed for a week.

8 Read the sentences. Some of them are correct and some have a word which should not be there. If a sentence is correct, put a tick next to it. If a sentence has a word which should not be there, write the word at the end of the line.

1 Rea can play the violin. ......✓......

2 Stop watching the TV and do your homework! ....

3 The Simpsons have bought a new house. ....

4 That ring is made of a gold. ....

5 We stayed at the Star Hotel. ....

6 Where can I find an information about this product? ....

7 There's a carton of milk in the fridge. ....

8 She was wearing a lovely blue dress. ....

9 We often play the tennis on Sundays. ....

10 The silence is golden. ....

9 Complete with *a/an, the* or – (zero article).

Internet facts and figures

(1) ....*The*.... Internet began as 'the Apranet' in 1969. Today, it is (2) .... fastest growing means of communication on (3) .... planet! Here are some facts about it.

- In 1997 there were 3.9 million people with access to the Internet in (4) .... Britain. By 1998, there were about 8 million!
- (5) .... very large number of college graduates in (6) .... USA find jobs through the Internet. After (7) .... English, (8) .... Japanese and (9) .... German are (10) .... languages that people use the most on the net.
- (11) .... Internet users are doubling in number every 100 days.
- (12) .... Americans spend more time using the Internet than reading (13) .... magazines or (14) .... newspapers.

10 Read and complete. Use *a/an, the* or – (zero article).

TeenLink
Bicycle History

by Anne Clark

The bicycle is (1) ....*a*.... very popular means of transport all over (2) .... world. But who invented it and how long has it been around? Last week I visited (3) .... Transport Museum to find out.

The first bicycle was designed in (4) .... Germany. In 1818, Baron Karl von Drais developed (5) .... machine which he called the 'dandy horse'. It was made of (6) .... wood and had no pedals – it was propelled by the rider's feet!

The first self-propelled bicycle was invented in (7) .... United Kingdom by (8) .... Kirkpatrick Macmillan, (9) .... blacksmith from (10) .... Scotland. It had (11) .... very large front wheel, because it was believed that this would make the bike faster.

The next development came about in the early 1880s, when the first 'safety bicycle' was invented. This invention became (12) .... model for the modern bicycle.

Oral practice Now you can do the **oral activity** for **Unit 13** (Teacher's Resource File).

Revision 9-13

1   Rewrite the sentences in the *passive*.

     0   We invited Jon to the party.
        Jon _was invited to the party._

     1   They say that his new book is better than the first one.
        His new book ....

     2   Fran Roberts is going to organise the reception.
        The reception ....

     3   They should restore that old building.
        That old building ....

     4   We will send you a report next week.
        You ....

     5   They haven't found the missing child yet.
        The missing child ....

     6   Many people believe that there is life on other planets.
        It ....

     7   Someone was following her on her way home.
        She ....

     8   They gave him a pay rise.
        He ....

     9   He made us tell him all about the secret formula.
        We ....

     10   Someone will have typed these letters by Monday.
        These letters ....

    (10)

2   Rewrite the sentences using the word given.

     0   Someone stole Bob's car last night. **had**
        Bob .... _had his car stolen_ .... last night.

     1   We must ask someone to fix that door as soon as possible. **have**
        We .... as soon as possible.

     2   Someone has photocopied the article for me. **had**
        I .... photocopied.

     3   Someone was painting their house when we spoke to them. **having**
        They .... when we spoke to them.

     4   Her secretary organises the meetings for her. **has**
        She .... her secretary.

     5   Did Julie Walters decorate your office? **have**
        Did you .... Julie Walters?

    (10)

3 Complete with the correct form of the verb.

Spending his free time in front of the TV was starting (0) ......*to get*...... (get) boring for Mick Richardson, a seventeen-year-old student from California. He was tired of (1) .... (go) out with friends and playing computer games, so he decided (2) .... (do) something more creative. He wrote a book!

'Wonderful World', Mick's first novel, was published a few months ago and it has already sold 5,000 copies in the USA.

'I was never particularly good at (3) ....,' (write) says Mick. 'I used (4) .... (be) a reporter for the school magazine but I had never thought of (5) .... (become) a writer! In fact, I was really surprised (6) .... (hear) that 'Wonderful World' was going to be published. It was too good (7) .... (be) true!'

Mick has already finished (8) .... (write) his second book. It's called 'Sparks' and it will (9) .... (be) published in less than a year. Don't forget (10) .... (buy) it when it comes out! We're sure you'll love it.

(10)

4 Rewrite the sentences using the word given.

0 The second half of the play wasn't as interesting as the first. **less**
The second half of the play ......*was less interesting than*...... the first.

1 I almost never eat meat. **hardly**
I .... meat.

2 She sings very well. **a**
She's .... singer.

3 Maria is shy and her friend is, too. **as**
Maria .... her friend.

4 If you try harder, you'll get better. **the**
The harder .... you'll get.

5 My CD player cost a lot but yours was more expensive. **much**
My CD player didn't .... yours.

(10)

5 Complete with *a, an, the* or – (zero article).

0 Who was the third president of ....*the*........ United States?
1 Lisa is in .... hospital with a broken leg.
2 It was .... hot day and the children were lying on the beach.
3 What time do you usually have .... dinner?
4 You shouldn't have stayed in .... sun for so long.
5 How long have you been learning .... English?
6 They say that .... love is blind.
7 Don't worry. This won't take more than .... hour.
8 Did you see .... van that just turned the corner?
9 I won't be .... home until nine.
10 You shouldn't work more than eight hours .... day.

(10)

Total (50)

Reported speech (1)
reported statements, commands and requests, questions

Dancing for her Life

by Josh Franklin

Fourteen-year-old Marianne Walters, a Year 10 student at our school, has won first prize in an international classical ballet competition!

I spoke to her the day after the competition and I asked her how she felt about her success. She told me that she had always dreamed of becoming a professional ballet dancer and added that she owed her success to her teacher, Ms Sheila Ross. She said that she had never been happier in her whole life.

Congratulations, Marianne! We're all very proud of you!

Grammar reference

A **Direct and reported speech**

We can use **direct speech** or **reported speech** to convey somebody's words.
▶ With **direct speech**, we convey the exact words that somebody said. The sentence that we are reporting goes in inverted commas and starts with a capital letter. Before or after this sentence, we use an reporting verb such as **say** or **tell**. The reporting verb and the speaker's words are separated by a comma.
He said, 'I'm very busy.'
'I have finished,' Mary told her teacher.

▶ With **reported speech**, we convey the general meaning of what somebody said, making some changes to his precise words. And here we use a reporting verb, but not in inverted commas. We can use the word **that** if we want
He said that he was very busy.
Mary told her teacher she had finished.

B Reported speech: statements

When we convert a sentence from **direct speech** into **reported speech**, we make some changes.

1 The **reporting verb** may change in some cases.

Direct speech	Reported speech
We use **say** when there is no indirect object, ie. when we do not refer to who said these words.	We use **say** when there is no indirect object, ie. when we do not refer to who said these words.
We use **say** to or **tell** when there is an object.	We use **tell** when there is an object.
Valerie **said**, 'I miss my sister.'	Valerie **said** (that) she missed her sister.
Valerie **said to me**, 'I miss my sister.'	Valerie **told me** (that) she missed her sister.
Valerie **told me**, 'I miss my sister.'	Valerie **told me** (that) she missed her sister.

2 **Pronouns** and **possessive adjectives** change according to the meaning of the sentence.

Brian said, 'I'm going to wear my new jacket.'
Brian said (that) he was going to wear his new jacket.

3 The **tenses of verbs** change when the reporting verb is in the **past tense**. The following table shows the changes that take place from **direct speech** into **reported speech** in all the tenses.

Direct speech	Reported speech
Present simple Alice said, 'I **hate** horror films.'	Past simple Alice said (that) she **hated** horror films.
Present continuous Mark said, '**I'm looking** for a new job.'	Past continuous Mark said (that) he **was looking** for a new job.
Past simple Erica said, 'Sam **arrived** at five.'	Past perfect simple Erica said (that) Sam **had arrived** at five.
Past continuous* Bill said, 'I **wasn't listening**.'	Past perfect continuous Bill said (that) he **hadn't been listening**.
Present perfect simple Lynne said, '**I've** never **ridden** a horse.'	Past perfect simple Lynne said (that) she **had** never **ridden** a horse.
Present perfect continuous Nigel said, '**I've been waiting** for hours.'	Past perfect continuous Nigel said (that) he **had been waiting** for hours.
Past perfect simple Megan said, 'I **had** already **left**.'	Past perfect simple Megan said (that) she **had** already **left**.
Past perfect continuous Stuart said, 'I **had been sleeping** for six hours.'	Past perfect continuous Stuart said (that) he **had been sleeping** for six hours.
will Clarissa said, '**I'll be** back at six.'	would Clarissa said (that) she **would be** back at six.
am/is/are going to Nick said, '**I'm going to have** a party.'	was/were going to Nick said (that) he **was going to have** a party.
can Zoe said, 'I **can't help** you.'	could Zoe said (that) she **couldn't help** me.
may Adam said, 'I **may be** late.'	might Adam said (that) he **might be** late.
must (obligation) Juliet said, 'I **must work** harder.'	had to Juliet said (that) she **had to work** harder.
needn't Charlie said, 'You **needn't call** her.'	needn't/didn't need to Charlie said (that) I **needn't/didn't need to call** her.
infinitive Lydia said, 'I want **to see** the film.'	infinitive Lydia said (that) she wanted **to see** the film.'

*The **past continuous** remains the same when we refer to an action or state that was under way in the past when something else happened.

He said, 'I was doing my homework when they arrived.'
He said (that) he was doing his homework when they arrived.

▶ The modal verbs **could, would, might, ought to, should** and **mustn't** do not change.

'I might see you later,' she told me.
She told me she might see me later.

▶ When **must** is used to express a logical conclusion, it does not change.

He said, 'They must be at home.'
He said they must be at home.

▶ The tenses of the verbs do not change:

• when the reporting verb is in the present tense or in the future tense.

She says, 'I'm not going to sell the house.'
She says she's not going to sell the house.

• when the sentence that we are reporting expresses a general truth or a fact that continues to apply.

He said, 'Buenos Aires is the capital of Argentina.'
He said Buenos Aires is the capital of Argentina.

In this case, it would not be incorrect to say He said Buenos Aires was the capital of Argentina, but it is not necessary to change the tense of the verb, and usually we do not.

• when the verb follows the expressions I wish or if only.

She said, 'I wish I had enough money for a new car.'
She said she wished she had enough money for a new car.

• when we have the second or third conditional in direct speech.

Sarah said, 'If I had the money, I would lend it to you.'
Sarah said that if she had the money, she would lend it to me.

George said, 'If I had been more careful, I would have passed the exam.'
George said that if he had been more careful, he would have passed the exam.

4 The **time markers** change.

Direct speech	Reported speech
now	then
today	that day
tonight	that night
this year	that year
yesterday	the day before, the previous day
a month ago	a month before
last week	the week before, the previous week
tomorrow	the next day, the following day
next year	the following year

Lesley told me, 'I'm meeting him tomorrow.'
Lesley told me she was meeting him the following day.

5 Some other words also change in **reported speech** according to the meaning of the sentence.

Direct speech	Reported speech
this/these	that/those
'This book is very interesting,' he said.	He said (that) **that** book was very interesting.
here	there
'I'll be **here** at five,' he said.	He said he'd be **there** at five.
come	go
'I won't **come** to the party,' she said.	She said she wouldn't **go** to the party.

Grammar practice

1 Complete with *said* or *told*.

> **Tip**
>
> Remember:
> She said, '...' → She said (that) ...
> She said to me, '...' → She told me (that) ...
> She told me, '...' → She told me (that) ...

1 Kate ......*said*...... Bill had won the lottery.

2 Mark .... me he was going to give her a ring for her birthday.

3 She ...., 'I haven't talked to Tim yet.'

4 He .... his boss that he had found a better job.

5 She .... to me, 'I'll never forgive you.'

6 Mum .... she'd be at the office until 5.30.

7 The security guard .... us that we couldn't enter the building.

8 'The test will begin in five minutes,' the teacher .... to the students.

2 Rewrite the sentences in *reported speech*.

1 My mother told us, 'I have been looking for my glasses all day.'
   My mother told us that she had been looking for her glasses all day.

2 'I don't understand,' Georgia said.
   ....

3 Sue told me, 'I saw Charles on my way to school.'
   ....

4 My brother told me, 'I'm not going to help you.'
   ....

5 She said to me, 'I've decided to move to a bigger house.'
   ....

6 'I need a new CD player,' he said.
   ....

7 I said, 'Stephen has already told me about the party.'
   ....

8 'Jack had been watching TV for hours!' she said.
   ....

9 She told me, 'I was working all day.'
   ....

10 Alex said, 'Bill is looking for a new job.'
   ....

11 'I've never been to Italy,' Mike said to me.
   ....

12 'No one was paying attention,' she said.
   ....

3 Rewrite the sentences in *reported speech*.

1 She said to me, 'You can borrow my camera.'
   She told me I could borrow her camera.

2 James said to Anne, 'You must call the police!'

3 I said to him, 'I can't help you.'
   ....

4 'I couldn't hear him,' she said.
   ....

5 He said, 'Lee must have forgotten about the meeting.'
   ....

6 'You should see a doctor,' he told me.
   ....

7 'My brother might still be in bed,' she said.
   ....

8 He said to Carol, 'You needn't get up early.'
   ....

9 My dad told me, 'You must stay at home.'
   ....

10 She said, 'The Smiths may move to London.'
   ....

11 'I would love to join you,' he told us.
   ....

12 She said, 'David must be tired.'
   ....

4 Read. Then rewrite the sentences in *reported speech*.

The Luck of the Draw
by Barbara Forbes

Last week Mr West, who teaches History and Geography at our school, became a very rich man! He won half a million pounds in a lottery. I managed to interview him as soon as I heard the news. This is what he told me:

'(1) I bought the winning ticket three weeks ago. (2) I saw the results of the draw in the newspaper yesterday. (3) This is not the first time someone in my family has won money. (4) My wife won £500 four years ago. (5) She is abroad, so she hasn't heard the good news yet. (6) She is returning from a business trip next week. (7) I'm going to collect my cheque tomorrow and buy my wife some diamond earrings. (8) I want to give her a surprise!'

1　Mr West said <u>that he had bought the winning ticket three weeks before.</u>
2　He said ....
3　He said ....
4　He said ....
5　He said ....
6　He said ....
7　He said ....
8　He said ....

5 Rewrite the sentences in *reported speech*.

1　He said, 'I'll never speak to him again if he doesn't apologise.'
　<u>He said he would never speak to him again if he didn't apologise.</u>

2　They told us, 'We'll be back next week.'
　...

3　Craig said, 'I've been trying to write this article since 8.30.'
　...

4　She told me, 'If you had been on time, we would have caught the bus.'
　...

5　Ethan said, 'I didn't have breakfast this morning.'
　...

6　'Paula was in her room a few minutes ago,' she said.
　...

7　'You can't park here,' the man told us.
　...

8　'If I didn't need the money, I would quit,' he told me.
　...

9　Diane said, 'Andy wasn't at the party last night.'
　...

10　The teacher told him, 'You ought to be more careful.'
　...

C Reported speech: commands and requests

▶ In order to convert orders and commands or requests into **reported speech**, the **imperative** that exists in **direct speech** changes into the **infinitive**.

Direct speech	Reported speech
She said to me, '**Listen** carefully.'	She told me **to listen** carefully.
'**Don't read** Anne's diary,' Alex said.	Alex told him **not to read** Anne's diary.
Amanda said, 'Please **go** away.'	Amanda asked them **to go** away.
He said, 'Please **don't make** a mess.'	He asked us **not to make** a mess.

▶ The reporting verbs that we usually use to convey a command or order are **tell** (tell) and **order** (order, command). We choose which of these two we will use according to the style and content of the sentence. We do not use say (to).

'Stop complaining,' Jim said to Lisa.
~~Jim said to Lisa to stop complaining.~~ ✗
Jim told Lisa to stop complaining.

'Answer my questions,' the judge said to the thief.
~~The judge said to the thief to answer her questions.~~ ✗
The judge ordered the thief to answer her questions.

▶ The reporting verbs that we usually use to convey a request are **ask** (ask) and **beg** (beg, beseech), again according to the style and content of the sentence. We do not use **say** (to). **Please** is omitted when we change the sentence into **reported speech**.

'Please let me read your article,' Charles said to Becky.
~~Charles said to Becky to let him read her article.~~ ✗
Charles asked Becky to let him read her article.

The little boy said, 'Please, please, don't switch off the light!'
~~The little boy said to his mother not to switch off the light.~~ ✗
The little boy begged his mother not to switch off the light.

---

6 Rewrite the sentences using the word given.

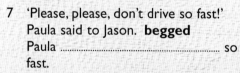

1 'Hurry up!' she said to him. **told**
   She .... _told him to hurry_ .... up.

2 He said, 'Don't make so much noise, Tom.' **told**
   He .... so much noise.

3 'Don't be afraid,' she told me. **to**
   She .... afraid.

4 'Give me the money!' the thief said to her. **ordered**
   The thief .... the money.

5 'Don't leave your toys on the floor,' she said to her son. **his**
   She told her son .... on the floor.

6 The teacher said to us, 'Read the instructions carefully.' **to**
   The teacher .... the instructions carefully.

7 'Please, please, don't drive so fast!' Paula said to Jason. **begged**
   Paula .... so fast.

8 Elsa said to Maggie, 'Please meet me at the station at six thirty.' **asked**
   Elsa .... at the station at six thirty.

9 He said to me, 'Don't worry.' **told**
   He .... worry.

10 'Follow that car!' the detective said to the driver. **ordered**
   The detective .... that car.

D

Reported speech: questions

▶ When we convert a question into **reported speech**, the syntax of the sentence changes. The verb in **reported speech** does not turn into a question, but into a positive form. The tenses of the verbs, the pronouns and time markers change, as in statements..
'Where are you going?' he asked me.
He asked me where I was going.

▶ If the question in **direct speech** starts with a **question word** (eg. **what, where, when, how**), the question in **reported speech** starts with the same word.
'Why are you crying, Jenny?' David asked.
David asked Jenny why she was crying.

▶ However, if the question in **direct speech** starts with an auxiliary verb (eg. **be, do, have**) or with a **modal verb**, the question in **reported speech** starts with the words **if** or **whether**.
'Did you post the letter?' she asked him. She asked him if/whether he had posted the letter.

▶ Some of the reporting verbs/expressions that we use are: **ask, wonder** and **want to know**.
'Where's Jack?' he asked.
He asked where Jack was.

'Why didn't he call?' she wondered.
She wondered why he hadn't called.

'Who are you talking to?' he asked.
He wanted to know who I was talking to.

---

7 Rewrite the questions in *reported speech*.

How often do you exercise?

1 'How often do you exercise?' the doctor asked him.
   The doctor asked him how often he exercised.

2 'Do you speak English?' the tourist asked us.
   ....

3 'When did he call?' she asked her mother.
   ....

4 Jeff asked her, 'Can you hear that noise?'
   ....

5 Emma asked Frank, 'Have you finished?'
   ....

6 'Where's the newspaper?' he asked me.
   ....

7 'Are the children still at school?' she asked him.
   ....

8 'How old are you?' she asked me.
   ....

9 He asked me, 'Did you have a good time?'
   ....

10 I asked her, 'What time does your train leave?'
   ....

11 'Is dinner ready?' she asked her mother.
   ....

12 'Why did you leave so early?' she asked him.
   ....

13 'Have you finished that article?' the boss asked him.
   ....

14 'When did Walter and Janet get married?' I asked her.
   ....

15 I asked Mum, 'Do you need any help?'
   ....

16 'Was the exam easy?' she asked us.
   ....

17 'What's your favourite colour?' he asked me.
   ....

18 'Will you help me?' she asked him.
   ....

8 Kiri Dean, the American pop star, is in London for a few days. Rewrite the reporters' questions in *reported speech*.

1 David Newton, *Daily News*: How long are you going to stay in London?
David asked how long she was going to stay in London.

2 May Enriques, *Chart Toppers*: Are you enjoying your stay?
May wanted to know ....

....

3 Steve Marsh, *Daily Gazette*: When are you going back to the USA?
Steve asked ....

4 Tanya Schiff, *Music Movers*: Is your husband travelling with you?
Tanya wanted to know ....

....

5 Jeff White, *The Belleville Herald*: When is your new CD coming out?
Jeff asked ....

....

6 Zenia North, *Fan Time*: How long did it take you to record your new CD?
Zenia wanted to know ....

....

7 Kim Lee, *Movers and Shakers*: Will you be giving any free concerts in London?
Kim wondered ....

8 Robin Young, *The Post*: Have you been to London before?
Robin asked ....

....

9 Rewrite the sentences in *direct speech*.

Remember::
In **direct speech**, the speaker's words go in inverted commas and are separated by a comma from the reporting verb.

1 He said he had never driven a car before.
He said, 'I have never driven a car before.'

2 I asked her if it was raining.
....

3 I told him to stop asking questions.
....

4 Diane said that the film had finished at nine.
....

5 The photographer asked us to stand still.
....

6 She said that she wanted to speak to Will.
....

7 The keeper told us not to feed the animals.
....

8 He said he couldn't sleep the night before.
....

9 The policeman asked her if the robbers had been wearing masks.
....

10 He asked us not to touch the exhibits.
....

E Reported speech: linking sentences

Sometimes, maybe we want to convert more than one sentence into **reported speech**. In this case, we can use words or phrases such as **and**, to join these sentences.
She told me, 'I'm tired. I'm going to bed.'
She told me she was tired and that she was going to bed.
She told me she was tired and added that she was going to bed.

14

10 Read. Then report what the critics said and link the sentences using the words given.

1

Simulation III

Reviewed by Teresa Williams

'Simulation III' is the most challenging game I've ever played. I'm sure action game fans will love it. (and)

Teresa Williams said that 'Simulation III' was the most challenging games he had ever played and she was sure that action game fans would love it.

2

Story Time by Stephen Allan
Reviewed by Miranda Robinson

'Story Time' is one of Stephen Allan's best books. Children will love this new collection of short stories. (added that)

3

SPACE TRAVELS,
directed by
Ellen La Commare
Reviewed by Bill Jones

Space Travels is an amazing science fiction film. The special effects are unbelievable! (and)

4

Wonderworld,
directed by George Baker
Reviewed by Harry Richards

I really enjoyed watching Wonderworld. George Baker is definitely a very talented director. (went on to say)

5

The Strangest Feeling
by Marjorie Wilde

Reviewed by Fred Clark

When I was a child, The Strangest Feeling was my favourite book. I really didn't expect the film to be as good as the book. (added that)

11 Rewrite the sentences using the word given.

1 'Have you fixed the computer?' I asked him. **if**
I asked him ____if he had fixed____ the computer.

2 He said to me, 'Lisa left yesterday.' **had**
He told me that _____ day.

3 'I'll see you at the office, Hugh,' she said. **told**
She _____ see him at the office.

4 'Did you see Dave at the party?' she asked me. **whether**
She asked me _____ Dave at the party.

5 'Please turn down the volume!' he said to them. **asked**
He _____ the volume.

6 'Will you be at my wedding?' she asked him. **he**
She asked him _____ at her wedding.

7 He said to me, 'I've never flown before.' **he**
He told me that _____ before.

8 He asked me, 'What did you buy for Kate's birthday?' **wanted**
He _____ I had bought for Kate's birthday.

USE OF ENGLISH
FCE

12 Read. Then report what Bruce Terry said using the words given.

Teen Link

by Sarah Thompson

An Interview with Bruce Terry

As you all know, Bruce Terry, the famous British film director has been in town, shooting his new film. Sarah Thomson was lucky enough to interview him for *Teen Link*!

Sarah: Mr Terry, how long have you been a director?

Mr Terry: (1) I have been a director for twenty-two years. (said) I have directed sixteen films. (and)

Sarah: Which is the most exciting film you have ever directed?

Mr Terry: (2) None of the films I've directed so far has been as exciting as 'Plateau'. (told) Working with so many talented actors has been a unique experience. (added that)

Sarah: Could you tell us a little about the making of your new film?

Mr Terry: (3) It takes a lot of hard work to make a film like 'Plateau'. (said) I really enjoy directing it. (but)

Sarah: Where did the idea for the film come from?

Mr Terry: (4) The film is based on a novel by D. K. Allan. (told) I wrote the script myself. (but)

Sarah: What will you do after you have finished this film?

Mr Terry: (5) Well, I have already started writing the script for 'Plateau II'. (said) My daughter Nancy is going to direct it.' (added that)

Sarah: Has your daughter ever directed a film before?

Mr Terry: (6) 'Plateau II' will be her first film. (told) I'm sure she's going to do a great job! (went on to say)

He said that he had been a director for twenty-two years and that he had directed sixteen films.

Writing practice Now you can do the **writing activity** for **Unit 14** (Teacher's Resource File).

He **agreed to take** me to the cinema. And I **promised that I wouldn't tell** you about his bad mark in the test!

Grammar reference

A Reporting verbs

Often in reported speech, we use some reporting verbs that express the speaker's tone and style. Most reporting verbs are formed using the infinitive, gerund or the word that. Some reporting verbs are formed in more than one way.

▶ reporting verb + infinitive

	Direct speech	Reported speech
agree	He said, 'All right. I'll lend you my camera.'	He **agreed to lend** me his camera.
demand	She said, 'I want to see the manager!'	She **demanded to see** the manager.
offer	He said, 'I'll help you.'	He **offered to help** me.
promise	She said, 'I'll be back soon.'	She **promised to be** back soon.
refuse	He said, 'No, I won't tell you my secret.'	He **refused to tell** me his secret.
threaten	She said, 'I'll tell Mum if you don't stop.'	She **threatened to tell** Mum if I didn't stop.

▶ **reporting verb + object + infinitive**

	Direct speech	Reported speech
advise	She said, 'You should get more sleep.'	She **advised me to get** more sleep.
beg	She said, 'Please lend me the money.'	She **begged me to lend** her the money.
forbid	He said, 'You can't see him again.'	He **forbade me to see** him again.
invite	She said, 'Will you join me?'	She **invited me to join** her.
order	He said, 'Don't move!'	He **ordered me not to move**.
remind	She said, 'Don't forget to post the letter.'	She **reminded me to post** the letter.
warn	She said, 'Don't press the button!'	She **warned me not to press** the button.

▶ **reporting verb + -ing**

	Direct speech	Reported speech
admit	He said, 'Yes, I stole the necklace.'	He **admitted stealing** the necklace.
deny	She said, 'No, I didn't read your diary.'	She **denied reading** my diary.

▶ **reporting verb + that**

	Direct speech	Reported speech
admit	She said, 'Yes, I **stole** the necklace.'	She **admitted that** she **had stolen** the necklace.
agree	He said, 'Yes, the film **is** excellent.'	He **agreed that** the film **was** excellent.
complain	She said, 'The hotel **is** too expensive.'	She **complained that** the hotel **was** too expensive.
deny	He said, 'No, I **didn't read** your diary.'	He **denied that he had read** my diary.
explain	She said, 'I **arrived** late because I **was** busy.'	She **explained that** she **had arrived** late because she **had been** busy.
inform	He said, 'You **have passed** the exam.'	He **informed me that** I **had passed** the exam.
promise	She said, 'I**'ll be** back soon.'	She **promised that** she **would be** back soon.
remind (somebody)	He said, '**Don't forget** that the guests **will arrive** at eight.'	He **reminded me that** the guests **would arrive** at eight.
threaten	She said, 'I**'ll tell** Mum if you **don't stop**.'	She **threatened that** she **would tell** Mum if I **didn't stop**.
warn (somebody)	He said, 'The water **is** dangerous.'	He **warned me that** the water **was** dangerous.

▶ **reporting verb + preposition + -ing**

accuse somebody of	She said, 'You **started** the fight!'	She **accused me of starting** the fight.
apologise for	He said, 'I'm sorry I **was** so selfish.'	He **apologised for being** so selfish.

▶ **suggest**
The verb **suggest** is formed in the following ways:

suggest + -ing	She said, '**Let's go** to the cinema.' She **suggested going** to the cinema.
suggest + that + past simple	She said, '**Let's go** to the cinema.' She **suggested that** we **went** to the cinema.
suggest + that + subject + should + infinitive without 'to'	She said, '**Let's go** to the cinema.' She **suggested that** we **should go** to the cinema.

15

Grammar practice

1 Rewrite the sentences using the word given.

1 'I can carry the suitcase for you,' Steve told me. (offered)
   Steve offered to carry the suitcase for me.

2 'I won't tell anyone,' Mary said. (promised)
   ....

3 'I'll call the police,' I said. (threatened)
   ....

4 'I'll come with you,' he told us. (agreed)
   ....

5 'I want to talk to your boss,' she told me. (demanded)
   ....

6 'No, I won't let you use my computer,' he said to me. (refused)
   ....

7 'I'll type that article for you,' she told me. (offered)
   ....

2 Rewrite the sentences using the word given.

1 'You should see a doctor,' he told her. (advised)
   He advised her to see a doctor.

2 'Don't go near the edge of the cliff!' I said to him. (warned)
   ....

3 'No, you can't go to the party,' my parents told me. (forbade)
   ....

4 'Stay with me, please,' Tricia said to Sarah. (begged)
   ....

5 'Give me your bag!' the thief told Diane. (ordered)
   ....

6 'Would you like to come to my party?' Harry said to me. (invited)
   ....

7 'Don't forget to tell Jane about the meeting,' he told me. (reminded)
   ....

3 Circle the correct answer.

1 Chris offered (to lend)/ lending me his car.

2 She warned her son not to play / playing with matches.

3 He denied to break / breaking the vase.

4 You promised to let / letting me wear your sweater!

5 He accused me of lie / lying.

6 Carol apologised for be / being late.

7 He refused to work / working on Sunday.

8 I suggested to have / having dinner at an Italian restaurant.

9 The policeman ordered her to answer / answering his question.

10 The boy admitted to break / breaking the window.

4 Rewrite the sentences.

1 He said to me, 'You told her my secret!'
   He accused me of telling her his secret.

2 She told me, 'I'm sorry I hurt your feelings.'
   She apologised ....

3 'I didn't do anything wrong!' I said.
   I denied ....

4 He told me, 'Yes, I lied to you.'
   He admitted ....

5 They told us, 'We're so sorry we didin't come to your party.'
   They apologised ....

6 'You took my sweater without asking me!' she said.
   She accused me ....

7 'I broke the window,' she said.
   She admitted ....

8 He said, 'I didn't steal the money!'
   He denied ....

9 She said to him, 'You are a selfish person!'
   She accused ....

10 I said to her, 'I am very sorry that I made you cry.'
   I apologised ....

5 Sue wasn't happy at work, so she talked to Mr Walker, her boss. Report what they said using the words given.

Sue

1 'I have started looking for a new job.' (informed)
Sue *informed Mr Walker that she had started looking for a new job.*

2 'My salary is too low.' (complained)
She ....

3 'I got my last pay rise three years ago.' (reminded)
She ....

Mr Walker

4 'You're right. You've been working very hard.' (agreed)
Mr Walker ....

5 'I've given you too many responsibilities.' (admitted)
He ....

6 'I'll give you a pay rise. (promised)
He ....

6 Rewrite each sentence in two different ways.

1 'Yes, I was responsible,' he said.
He admitted *that he had been responsible.*
He admitted *being responsible.*

2 'Why don't we invite Dave?' she said.
She suggested ....
She suggested ....

3 'I'll look after the baby,' I said.
I promised ....
I promised ....

4 'No, I didn't cause the accident,' the man said.
The man denied ....
The man denied ....

5 'I'll report you to the police,' she said to him.
She threatened ....
She threatened ....

6 'Don't forget that you have to be back by seven,' he told me.
He reminded me ....
He reminded me ....

7 Rewrite the sentences using the word given

USE OF
FCE
ENGLISH

1 'Yes, I was wrong,' he said. **that**
He admitted ...*that he had been*... wrong.

2 'Don't go fishing in such bad weather,' she told us. **warned**
She .... fishing in such bad weather.

3 'Why don't we have something to eat?' he said. **having**
He .... eat.

4 'You can leave school earlier on Tuesday,' Ms Smith told her students. **that**
Ms Smith promised her students .... school earlier on Tuesday.

5 'You shouldn't stay up so late,' he told me. **advised**
He .... up so late.

6 'I'm sorry I broke your CD,' I told her. **for**
I .... her CD.

7 'No, I didn't cheat in the exam!' he said. **that**
He denied .... in the exam.

8 'Why don't you stay a bit longer?' she told us. **invited**
She .... a bit longer.

Oral practice Now you can do the **oral activity** for **Unit 15** (Teacher's Resource File).

Relative clauses

defining and non-defining relative clauses, contact clauses, coordinate relative clauses

Teen Link

Shakespeare's Birthplace

by Suzanne Marshall

William Shakespeare was born in Stratford-on-Avon, in 1564. He spent his childhood in a house in Henley Street, **which** is now one of the town's most famous landmarks. The old farmhouse **where** Britain's greatest playwright was born was built in the 16ᵗʰ century. It originally belonged to Shakespeare's father, **who** was one of Stratford's most successful businessmen. The house has been open to the public since 1847, **when** it was bought by the Shakespeare Birthplace Trust.

Grammar reference

A   Relative pronouns

Relative clauses are introduced by a **relative pronoun**. The relative pronouns are:
▶ who (who) for people.
▶ whom (whom) for people.
▶ which (which) for things or animals.
▶ that (that) for people, animals or things, used more in oral speech than who, whom, or which.
▶ whose (whose) for people, animals or things.
▶ where (where).
▶ when (when).
▶ why (why).
The man whose car was stolen called the police.
The restaurant where they had dinner was very expensive.

Grammar practice

1 Complete with *who, which, whose, where, when* or *why*.

1 The man ......who...... called didn't leave a message.

2 Did you see the letter .... came for you this morning?

3 The shop .... she works is in Cherry Street.

4 Do you remember the day .... you first met?

5 The woman .... car was stolen went to the police station.

6 Is that the reason .... she got angry?

7 I don't know the girl .... is having the party.

8 This is the restaurant .... we had dinner last night.

9 The book .... I'm reading at the moment is a historical novel.

10 The boy .... brother is a tennis champion is in our class.

B Defining relative clauses

▶ The **relative pronouns** that are used in **defining relative clauses** are:

who/that	The man **who/that works in this shop** is Tim's father.
whom/that	The boy **whom/that we met at the party** is Jill's cousin.
which/that	The keys **which/that are on the table** are mine.
whose	She is an artist **whose paintings are very popular**.
where	The village **where he lives** is quite near Brighton.
when/that	That was the day **when/that I met** Charles.
why/that	This is not the reason **why/that I called**.

▶ **Defining relative clauses** provide the information that is necessary in a clause. Without this, the clause would not have a complete meaning. Look at the example:
The woman who used to live next door has moved to Scotland.
If we leave out the **defining relative clause,** only the main clause remains: … The defining relative clause, ie. who used to live next door, is necessary for the clause to have a complete meaning. It answers the question: Which woman?

---

2 Join the sentences using a *relative pronoun*.

1 The girl said she wanted to speak to Tim. She called.
   The girl who called said she wanted to speak to Tim.

2 The men have been arrested. They robbed the bank.
   ....

3 The car has been repaired. It was damaged in the accident.
   ....

4 That's the book shop. Lisa's sister works there.
   ....

5 The cheese sandwiches are for you. They're on the kitchen table.
   ....

6 An old lady called the fire brigade. Her cat had got stuck in a tree.
   ....

7 Do you remember the day? We first came to this school then.
   ....

8 The woman smiled proudly. Her daughter won first prize.
   ....

9 The architect is from Sweden. He designed this building.
   ....

10 The painting cost me £1,000. It is hanging on the sitting room wall.
   ....

C Contact clauses

▶ When the **relative pronoun** is the object of the **defining relative clause**, then usually we omit it. We thus convert the **defining relative clause** into a **contact clause**.
- She's the girl. I met her at the party.
- She's the girl who/whom/that I met at the party.
- She's the girl I met at the party.

▶ When the **relative pronoun** is the object of the **defining relative clause**, it cannot be omitted.
- I talked to the man. He owns the shop.
- I talked to the man who/that owns the shop.

▶ **Whose** is never omitted.
That's the girl. Her father is a famous artist.
That's the girl whose father is a famous artist.

▶ When/that can be omitted.
Was that the year? You finished school then.
Was that the year when/that you finished school?
Was that the year you finished school?

▶ Why/that can be omitted.
This is the reason. I didn't accept the job.
This is the reason why/that I didn't accept the job.
This is the reason I didn't accept the job.

3 Join the sentences with a *contact clause*.

Tip

Remember:
The **relative pronoun** can only be omitted when it is the object of the clause.

1 Thank you very much for the postcard. You sent it to me from Paris.
Thank you very much for the postcard you sent me from Paris.

2 The man was Wayne's grandfather. We saw him at the bus stop.

3 That's the boy. His ball broke our window.

4 The bus goes to London. It leaves from here.

5 Where's the envelope? I had left it on my desk.

6 The woman is an actress. She is standing next to Lee.

7 We visited the house. Davina Richards lived there for twenty-five years.

8 This is the job. I've always wanted it!

9 Show me the shirt. You bought it for Lisa's birthday.

10 The thieves were arrested. They robbed the National Bank.

11 The girl is my new classmate. Her parents are standing over there.

12 The shirt doesn't fit. Dan gave it to me.

13 I haven't read the book. You recommended it.

14 We know the woman. She is making the speech tonight.

D   **Prepositions in relative clauses**

► In **relative clauses**, prepositions may go before or after **relative pronouns**. Usually, and particularly in *everyday* speech, we put the preposition after the **relative pronoun** at the end of the **relative clause**. In this case, the **relative pronoun** can be omitted.
That's the boy. She was speaking to him.
That's the boy (who/whom/that) she was speaking to.

► Prepositions can also go before the **relative pronouns whom** and **which**. But this is quite formal and is not usual in everyday speech. Please note that we cannot use a preposition before **who** or **that**.
The man is a doctor. We sold our house to him.
The man (who/whom/that) we sold our house to is a doctor.
~~**The man to who/that we sold our house is a doctor.**~~   ✗
The man to whom we sold our house is a doctor.

► Please also note the following examples.
This is the house. Jane Stewart was born there.
This is the house where Jane Stewart was born.

This is the house. Jane Stewart was born in it.
This is the house in which Jane Stewart was born.
This is the house Jane Stewart was born in.

---

4   Join the sentences in two different ways.

> We can use a preposition before **whom** and **which**.

I   I don't know anyone. You can sell your car to them.
I don't know anyone to whom you can sell your car.
I don't know anyone you can sell your car to.

2   This is the hotel. We stayed at this hotel last year.

....

....

3   This is the restaurant. We usually go to it.

....

....

4   She's the woman. I borrowed the money from her.

....

....

5   That's the room. She spends most of her time in it.

....

....

6   History is a subject. I've always been good at it.

....

....

7   She's the friend. I share all my secrets with her.

....

....

8   This is the box. Mum keeps her jewellery in it.

....

....

E   Non-defining relative clauses

▶ The **relative pronouns** that we use in **non-defining relative clauses** are:

who	Albert Einstein, **who was a great scientist,** loved playing the violin.
who/whom	The Smiths, **who/whom you met last summer**, are visiting us again this year.
which	The African elephant, **which is the largest land mammal**, is in danger of extinction.
whose	Mr and Mrs Jackson, **whose son is my best friend**, are coming to dinner tonight.
where	I would love to visit France, **where my mother was born**.
when	She was born in 1969, **when the first astronauts landed on the moon.**

▶ **Non-defining relative clauses** provide additional information about somebody or something. They are not necessary in a clause in order for it to have a complete meaning.
Agatha Christie, who was born in 1890, wrote 'The Mousetrap'.
The meaning of the clause would have been completed if we had said Agatha Christie wrote 'The Mousetrap'.
The **non-defining relative clause** simply provides further information.

▶ **Non-defining relative clauses** always go between two commas when they are in the middle of the clause.
My brother, who lives in Bristol, is a teacher.

▶ If the **non-defining relative clause** is at the end of the clause, we put a comma before it.
I asked Mary, who said she had no idea what was going on.

▶ **Relative pronouns** cannot be left out of **non-defining relative clauses**.
This coat, which I bought three years ago, cost a lot of money.
~~This coat, I bought three years ago, cost a lot of money.~~ ✗

▶ In non-defining relative clauses, that cannot be replaced by who or which.
This building, which used to be a school, was built 500 years ago.
~~This building, that used to be a school, was built 500 years ago.~~ ✗

5 Join the sentences with a *non-defining relative clause*.

1 Jane Brown got married last week. She used to work for our company.
Jane Brown, who used to work for our company, got married last week.

2 My brother is a vet. He lives in France.

3 His new book will be published in March. It's called 'Congo Drums'.

4 Carol is my neighbour. Her father teaches English at my school.

5 Milan is a beautiful city. We spent our holidays there.

6 The year 1996 was the happiest year of my life. I met my husband then.

7 That building is a hotel. It is more than a hundred years old.

8 Robert speaks excellent English. He has never been to England.

9 Kevin was in a very bad mood. His car had been stolen.

10 The ABC Theatre was full last night. It holds more than a thousand people.

11 Mick was here ten minutes ago. You met him last week.

12 This postcard is from Paris. My parents are staying there.

13 Mr and Mrs Harris moved to London last year. They used to live next door.

14 Their house was damaged in the earthquake. It is rather old.

F **Coordinate relative clauses**
▶ **Which** can refer to a complete clause. In this case, the relative clause is called a **coordinate relative clause** and we put a comma before it.
I had been waiting for two hours. This made me very angry!
I had been waiting for two hours, which made me very angry!

6 Join the sentences using *a coordinate relative clause.*

I Jane didn't even say hello. This was very rude of her.
Jane didn't even say hello, which was very rude of her.

2 Bob didn't pass the exam. This made his parents very angry.
....

3 He says he has met the Prime Minister. This can't be true.
....

4 I've been working all day. This is why I feel so tired.
....

5 She is more than two hours late. This is very annoying.
....

6 Mary had a fight with Nick. This explains why she looks so upset.
....

7 Gavin gave me a watch for my birthday. This was very kind of him.
....

8 It's their anniversary. This is why they're having the party.
....

7 Read and complete. Use only one word in each space.

Charlie Chaplin
by Sarah Watts

Charlie Chaplin, (1) ......*whose*...... full name was Charles Spencer Chaplin, was one of the most talented comedians of all time. The little man (2) .... made thousands of people laugh was born in London on 16 April 1889. Chaplin, (3) .... parents were music hall entertainers, started his career very early in life. He made his first stage appearance in 1894, (4) .... he was only five years old.
In 1910 he left England and moved to the USA, (5) .... he made most of his films. His first film, (6) .... was called 'Making a Living', was made in 1914.

Chaplin, (7) .... was also a very talented director and composer, appeared in more than 80 films.

In 1952 he moved to Switzerland, (8) .... he spent the rest of his life with his wife Oona O'Neil and their children.

Chaplin's last film, (9) .... was called 'A Countess from Hong Kong', was made in 1967.

The king of silent comedy died on 25 December 1977.

Writing practice Now you can do the **writing activity** for **Unit 16** (Teacher's Resource File).

Clauses

'in case', clauses of purpose, result, reason, concession, contrast

TeenLink

Puzzle Zone

Here are this week's cool puzzles.
Can you solve them?

by Chris Bower

1 A scarf, five buttons and a carrot are lying on the lawn. Nobody put them there **but** there is a perfectly logical reason why they're there. What is it?

2 I left my house this morning **in order to** go shopping. **Although** I didn't have an umbrella or a raincoat, I didn't get wet. Why not?

3 **In spite of** winning the race, Sally didn't get a medal. Why not?

4 I went to the station **to** pick up a doctor, a teacher and a lawyer. **Although** I knew that one of them was called David, I had never met any of these people before. **However**, I identified David immediately. How?

Answers

1 Some children used them **in order to** make a snowman. The snow melted, **so** now they're lying on the lawn.

2 I didn't get wet **because** it wasn't raining.

3 Sally is a horse.

4 It was easy to identify David **because** he was the only man.

Grammar reference

A	in case

The phrase **in case** means 'in case'

in case + present tense (when we refer to the present or the future)	I'll stay at home in case she calls.
in case + past tense (when we refer to the past)	I stayed at home in case she called.

B   **Clauses of purpose**

▶ **Clauses of purpose** express purpose and are introduced by various words or phrases.

í When we have same subject, ie. when the subject of the main clause is the same as the subject of the **clause of purpose, in order not to** and **so as not to.**

• In positive clauses, we can use:

to + infinitive (to)	She left early to catch the train.
in order to + infinitive (in order to, so as to)	She left early in order to catch the train.
so as to + infinitive (so as to)	She left early so as to catch the train.

• In negative clauses, we can use:

in order not to + infinitive (in order not to, so as not to)	She left early in order not to miss the train.
so as not to + infinitive (in order not to, so as not to))	She left early so as not to miss the train.

• But we cannot use **not to.**
~~She left early not to miss the train.~~ ✗

▶ When we have a different subject, ie. when the subject of the main clause is different from the subject of the **clause of purpose,** we use **so that** or **in order that.**

so that + subject + can/will (so that) (when we refer to the present or the future)	I'll give her my phone number so that she can contact me. I'll talk to him so that he'll know what to do.
so that + subject + could/would (so that) (when we refer to the past)	I gave her my phone number so that she could contact me. I talked to him so that he would know what to do.
in order that + subject + can/will (so that, to) (when we refer to the present or the future)	I'll give her my phone number in order that she can contact me. I'll talk to him in order that he'll know what to do.
in order that + subject + could/would (so that, to) (when we refer to the past)	I gave her my phone number in order that she could contact me. I talked to him in order that he would know what to do.

▶ **In order that** and **so that** may also be used when the subject is the same. However, in this case, we have to refer to the subject again.
She is leaving early so that she can catch the train.
She left early so that she could catch the train.

17

Grammar practice

1 Join the sentences using *in case*.

Diane's friends are coming to her house this evening. They're going to watch a video. Diane has made a list of the things she needs to do.

1 I'll ask Dad about the video. He might not have fixed it yet.
   I'll ask Dad about the video in case he hasn't fixed it yet.

2 I'll rent a comedy. Tina might not like horror films.

3 I'll make some sandwiches. We might get hungry.

4 I'll call Mike. He might not remember about tonight.

5 I'll give Wanda a ring. She might want to join us.

2 Join the sentences using *in case*.

1 Take an umbrella with you. It might rain.
   Take an umbrella with you in case it rains.

2 I took an umbrella with me. I thought it might rain.

3 She is doing the exercise carefully. Otherwise she may make a mistake.

4 We'd better phone them. They may be out.

5 I didn't laugh. I didn't want to hurt her feelings.

6 Rick always takes some money with him. He might need it.

3 Join the sentences using the words given.

1 He went to Bristol. He wanted to visit his grandparents. (in order to)
   He went to Bristol in order to visit his grandparents.

2 She worked late. She wanted to finish the article on time. (so as to)

3 I went to the supermarket. I wanted to get some orange juice. (to)

4 We're going to book tickets. We don't want to miss the concert. (in order not to)

5 He's been training hard. He wants to win the race. (so as to)

6 They went for a walk. They wanted to get some fresh air. (to)

7 He's saving up. He wants to visit Canada in July. (in order to)

8 He didn't tell her about the accident. He didn't want to upset her. (so as not to)

130

4 Join the sentences using the words given.

1 He spoke loudly. He wanted everyone to hear him. (in order that)
   He spoke loudly in order that everyone could hear him.

2 I am leaving the note on the kitchen table. John will see it when he gets back. (so that)
   ....
   ....

3 Give them your address. They can send you the contract. (in order that)
   ....
   ....

4 She wanted to get good marks. She didn't want her parents to be disappointed. (so that)
   ....
   ....

5 Take a map of the city. We don't want to get lost. (in order that)
   ....
   ....

6 I'll leave him a message. He won't wonder where I am. (so that)
   ....
   ....

7 I've washed your blue dress. You can wear it at the party tomorrow. (so that)
   ....
   ....

8 She hid her diary. She didn't want her mother to find it. (in order that)
   ....
   ....

9 I'll post the letter tomorrow. It will get there by next week. (so that)
   ....
   ....

10 Alice did all the housework. She wanted her mother to get some rest. (so that)
   ....
   ....

11 Andy gave me some money. He wanted me to buy a newspaper. (in order that)
   ....
   ....

12 She always locks her office. Nobody can get inside. (so that)
   ....
   ....

5 Join the sentences using *in order (not) to/so as (not) to* or *in order that/so that*.

Tip

Remember that **in order (not) to** and **so as (not) to** are only used when the subject is the same.

In order that and **so that** are used when the subject is the same or different.

1 They lit a fire. They wanted to keep warm.
   They lit a fire in order to keep warm.

2 I bought some more popcorn. We wanted to have enough for the party.
   ....

3 I'm going to the bank. I want to ask for a loan.
   ....

4 Myra wrote down Valerie's address. She didn't want to forget it.
   ....

5 He took a taxi. He wanted to get there on time.
   ....

6 We turned down the music. We didn't want the neighbours to start complaining.
   ....

7 Close the window. I don't want the cat to go out.
   ....

8 Francis took off his shoes. He didn't want to make any noise.
   ....

131

C Clauses of result

▶ Clauses of result express a result and are introduced by various words or phrases.

so + clause (so, consequently)	I was tired, so I went straight to bed.
so + adjective/adverb + that (so...that)	I was so busy that I forgot to call him. She spoke so quickly that I couldn't understand what she was saying.
such a/an + adjective + singular noun + that (such a/an...that)	It was such a funny story that we couldn't stop laughing.
such + adjective + plural/uncountable noun (such...that)	They're such nice people that everyone likes them. We're having such awful weather that we can't go swimming.

▶ We use **so** with the words **much, many, little** and **few**. We use **such** with the phrase **a lot of**.

so + much + uncountable noun + that	There was so much noise that we couldn't hear him.
so + many + countable noun + that	There were so many people at the cinema that I couldn't find a seat.
so + little + uncountable noun + that	There was so little air in the room that we couldn't breathe.
so + few + countable noun + that	He made so few mistakes that the teacher gave him an 'A'.
such + a lot of + uncountable/countable noun + that	She made such a lot of noise that she woke everyone up.

▶ To express the result of an action, we can also use **therefore, consequently, as a result** (consequently, and so).
He didn't study and therefore/consequently/as a result he failed the test.
He didn't study. Therefore/Consequently/As a result, he failed the test.

D Clauses of reason

Clauses of reason express the cause or the reason why something is happening and are introduced by various words or phrases.

because + clause (since, because)	The bus arrived late because the traffic was heavy. Because the traffic was heavy, the bus arrived late.
because of + noun/pronoun (because of)	The bus arrived late because of the heavy traffic. Because of the heavy traffic, the bus arrived late.
because of the fact that + clause (because of the fact that)	The bus arrived late because of the fact that the traffic was heavy. Because of the fact that the traffic was heavy, the bus arrived late.
as/since + clause (because, since)	The bus arrived late as/since the traffic was heavy. As/Since the traffic was heavy, the bus arrived late.
due to + noun (due to)	The bus arrived late due to the heavy traffic. Due to the heavy traffic, the bus arrived late.
on account of + noun (due to)	The bus arrived late on account of the heavy traffic. On account of the heavy traffic, the bus arrived late.
due to/on account of the fact that + clause (due to the fact that)	The bus arrived late due to/on account of the fact that the traffic was heavy. Due to/On account of the fact that the traffic was heavy, the bus arrived late.

6 Rewrite the sentences using the word given.

Tip

We usually put a comma before **so**.

We do not usually put a comma before **because**.

1 I had a terrible headache, so I took an aspirin. (because)

   I took an aspirin because I had a terrible
   headache.

2 We couldn't get in because I had forgotten my keys. (so)

   ....

3 They called the police because they were worried. (so)

   ....

4 She had been waiting for three hours, so she was angry. (because)

   ....

5 He asked for my help because he couldn't do it by himself. (so)

   ....

6 I don't speak French, so I can't understand what she's saying. (because)

   ....

7 I don't know anything about Biology, so I can't help you. (because)

   ....

7 Complete with *because* or *because of*.

Tip

Because is followed by a clause.
Because of is followed by a noun, pronoun or proper name.

1 He won't be playing on Sunday *because* he has broken his leg.

2 I couldn't concentrate .... the noise.

3 She didn't tell him about it .... she doesn't trust him.

4 Everything went wrong .... a silly mistake.

5 He had to leave .... an emergency.

6 I didn't buy the shirt .... it was too small.

7 They cancelled their trip .... the fact that it was snowing.

8 I turned off the television .... no one was watching it.

9 She didn't accept the job .... the salary was too low.

10 I lost my job .... you!

8 Rewrite the sentences using the word given.

USE OF ENGLISH

1 Nobody likes him because he's so selfish. **fact**
   Nobody likes him *because of the fact*
   that he's so selfish.

2 She didn't attend the meeting because she was ill. **of**
   She didn't attend the meeting ....
   .... her illness.

3 He's angry because of what you said about Thomas. **account**
   He's angry .... what you said about Thomas.

4 We stayed at home because of the rain. **fact**
   We stayed at home because ....
   .... was raining.

5 Our flight was delayed because of the thick fog. **account**
   Our flight was delayed ....
   the thick fog.

6 The meeting was cancelled because the manager was absent. **fact**
   The meeting was cancelled ....
   .... that the manager was absent.

7 We succeeded because you helped us. **fact**
   Due .... you helped us, we succeeded.

133

17

9 Complete with *so*, *such* or *such a/an*.

> **Tip**
>
> **So** is followed by an adjective or an adverb.
> **Such a/an** is followed by a singular noun.
> **Such** is followed by a plural noun or by an uncountable noun.
> We use **so** before **much**, **many**, **few** and **little**, and **such** before **a lot of**.

1 I was ......*so*....... angry that I started shouting at her.

2 It was .... boring film that we left before the end.

3 He drove .... fast that we got there in five minutes.

4 It was .... cold weather that we decided not to go swimming.

5 She was .... disappointed that she started crying.

6 There were .... a lot of people at the cinema that I couldn't find a seat.

7 They're .... good friends that they share all their secrets.

8 Bob ate .... much ice cream that he had a stomach ache afterwards.

9 I had .... little money that I couldn't even buy my train ticket.

10 Dora has .... wonderful memories of her trip to Holland that she's going back there next year.

10 Join the sentences using *so ... that*, *such a/an ... that* or *such ... that*.

1 She's read many books about ancient Greece. She knows a lot about the subject.
   She's read so many books about ancient Greece that she knows a lot about the subject.

2 He got bad marks. His parents were furious.
   ....

3 I'm hungry. I could eat a horse!
   ....

4 I've got a lot of work to do. I won't be able to come with you.
   ....

5 She felt embarrassed. She didn't know what to say.
   ....

6 It was an interesting book. I couldn't put it down.
   ....

7 He speaks English well. Nobody can believe he's really French.
   ....

8 There was heavy traffic. I was almost an hour late.
   ....

9 We were having a good time. We didn't want to leave.
   ....

10 This exercise is difficult. I can't do it by myself.
   ....

II Read and complete. Use only one word in each space.

What does exercise mean for your **body?**

by Paula James

A lot of things happen to your body when you exercise. In any type of exercise, your muscles start working harder (1) _because_ they must keep your body moving. As you exercise, your body does many things in (2) .... to meet the needs of working muscles. Your heart, for example, beats faster so as (3) .... pump more blood to the muscles. Your lungs need to absorb more oxygen, (4) .... you start breathing faster. Some other systems shut down in order (5) .... to waste energy that your muscles need.

All these processes require a lot of energy. But where does this energy come from?

Well, your body produces a substance called ATP, which it uses (6) .... keep your muscles moving. ATP is (7) .... important that without it every muscle in your body would stop moving.

Exercise means a lot of hard work for your body but it is so good for you (8) .... it's really worth the effort!

E Clauses of concession

We use **clauses of concession** to refer to how something is happening, despite the fact that something else is influencing it. **Clauses of concession** are introduced by various words or phrases.

but + clause (but)	She was tired but she offered to help me.
however + clause (however, despite that)	She was tired. However, she offered to help me. She was tired. She offered to help me, however.
although/even though/though + clause (although, despite the fact that)	Although/Even though/Though she was tired, she offered to help me. She offered to help me although/even though/though she was tired.
in spite of/despite + noun (despite + noun)	In spite of/Despite her tiredness, she offered to help me. She offered to help me in spite of/despite her tiredness.
in spite of/despite + –ing (in spite of)	In spite of/Despite being tired, she offered to help me. She offered to help me in spite of/despite being tired.
in spite of/despite + the fact that + clause (despite the fact that)	In spite of/Despite the fact that she was tired, she offered to help me. She offered to help me in spite of/despite the fact that she was tired.

135

F	Clauses of contrast

Clauses of contrast express contrast and are introduced by various words or phrases.

while + clause (while)	He loves comedies while his wife hates them.
whereas + clause (whereas)	I felt like going out whereas Tom wanted to stay at home.
on the other hand + clause (on the other hand)	I think jogging is rather boring. On the other hand, it's a good way to keep fit.

12 Rewrite the sentences using the word given.

1 In spite of the fact that we left early, we missed our bus. **leaving**
In spite of ....leaving early........, we missed our bus.

2 Despite her parents' objections, she went to the party. **of**
In ...., she went to the party.

3 I went out in spite of the fact that I was exhausted. **being**
In ...., I went out.

4 Despite being in a hurry, I remembered to lock the door. **fact**
Despite .... in a hurry, I remembered to lock the door.

5 We had a great time in spite of the fact that he complained. **complaints**
In spite ...., we had a great time.

6 She was wearing a jacket in spite of the fact that it was hot. **heat**
In spite ...., she was wearing a jacket.

7 Despite the fact that she tried hard, she failed the exam. **trying**
In ...., she failed the exam.

8 Despite knowing the answer, she refused to help me. **fact**
In spite of .... the answer, she refused to help me.

9 He wasn't promoted despite the fact that he worked hard. **working**
In ...., he wasn't promoted.

10 Despite the fact that he was strong, he couldn't move the table. **being**
Despite ...., he couldn't move the table.

13 Rewrite the sentences using the words given.

1 In spite of getting up late, we managed to get there on time. (although)
Although we got up late, we managed to get there on time.

2 In spite of feeling guilty, she didn't apologise. (although)
....

3 He went on working, although he had a terrible headache. (in spite of)
....

4 They went shopping in spite of the bad weather. (although)
....

5 I ate the cake although I wasn't hungry. (in spite of)
....

6 I went to the concert in spite of the fact that I hate pop music. (although)
....

7 Although she's the boss, she works as hard as we do. (in spite of)
....

8 In spite of the fact that he lies to her, she trusts him. (although)
....

9 Although she isn't a very good student, she did well in the test. (in spite of)
....

10 Although he knew he was wrong, he refused to admit it. (in spite of)
....

11 In spite of having problems, she's always cheerful. (although)
....

12 Although I enjoyed the film, I don't want to see it again. (in spite of)
....

14 Join the sentences with *and* or *while/whereas*.

> **Tip**
>
> We join two similar clauses with **and**. We simply add something else to that which is expressed in the first clause.
> With **while/whereas**, we join two clauses that have contrasting meanings. We add a clause that is contrary to what the first expresses.

1 I love walking to work every morning. My wife always takes the bus.
   I love walking to work every morning whereas my wife always takes the bus.

2 I went to the library this morning. I saw Nick there.
   ....

3 She looked at me. She smiled.
   ....

4 He usually watches TV in his free time. I prefer listening to music.
   ....

5 Bob called. He said he'd be back at eight.
   ....

6 Her first book wasn't very good. Her second one has already sold 5,000 copies.
   ....

7 He ran fast. He won the race easily.
   ....

8 I loved the film. Anne found it rather boring.
   ....

9 She earns £40,000 a year. He only makes about £15,000.
   ....

10 We met five years ago. We've been good friends ever since.
   ....

15 Read and complete. Use only one word in each space.

FLYING HIGH:
The exciting sport of Hang-gliding
by Timothy Smith

You've probably heard of hang-gliding (1) ....*but*.... have you ever wondered how a hang-glider actually works?

How do they fly?

(2) .... order to fly, people use a special type of parachute, which looks like a kite. It's in the shape of a triangle so (3) .... the air can flow over its surface more easily (4) .... make it rise. (5) .... start flying, the pilot must run down a slope, so (6) .... to let the air flow over the hang-glider's surface.

Is it safe?

Yes, it is. (7) ...., it is always good to check your equipment before each flight in order (8) .... make sure that everything is in good condition. Many people also carry a reserve parachute (9) .... case something goes wrong. (You never know!)

A unique experience

(10) .... the idea of hang-gliding may sound rather frightening, the feeling is great! Fans of the sport say that it can be (11) .... an amazing experience that you soon get over your fears.

> **Writing practice** Now you can do the **writing activity** for **Unit 17** (Teacher's Resource File).

Prepositions

prepositions of time, place, movement,
dependent prepositions

No, Daddy. Mummy can't come **to** the phone **at** the moment. But don't worry **about** your message. She'll see it.

Grammar reference

A Prepositions of time

Prepositions of time indicate time.
We use:

▶ **at**
- for the time: **at eight o'clock**
- with expressions: **at Christmas/Easter, at noon/midday/night/midnight, at breakfast/ lunch/dinner, at the weekend, at the moment, at present**

▶ **on**
- with days of the week: **on Monday**
- for part of a specific day: **on Friday evening, on Monday morning**
- with dates: **on 9th August**
- with expressions: **on a hot/cold day, on Christmas Eve, on New Year's Day, on my birthday**

▶ **in**
- with centuries: **in the twentieth century, in the sixteenth century**
- with years: **in 1998, in 2002**
- with seasons: **in spring, in the summer**
- with months: **in March, in September**
- with expressions: **in the morning, in the afternoon, in the evening**

▶ **by, until**
- The preposition **by** means 'by', 'not later than'.
  You must be back by midnight.
- The preposition **until** means 'until'.
  You can keep my car until Monday.
  By and **until** are not used in the same way.
  With **by**, we refer to something that will take place (at the latest) by some time in the future. With **until**, we refer to the duration that an action or state will have.
  Compare the examples below:
  I'll be at the office by eight. (I will get to the office by eight at the latest.)
  I'll be at the office until eight. (I will be at the office until eight. Then I will leave.)

▶ **during**
The preposition **during** means 'during' and is always followed by a noun.
You must be quiet during the lesson.
During is used in the same way as **while**. **While** is not a preposition and is followed by a clause. Compare the following examples.
- **during + noun**
  Mary fell asleep during the film.
- **while + clause**
  Mary fell asleep while she was watching the film.

Grammar practice

1 Complete with *at, on* or *in*.

1 Our train leaves ......*at*...... half past seven.

2 He'll be back .... Friday afternoon.

3 Nellie and Jarvis are getting married .... September.

4 I always send her a card .... Christmas.

5 A lot of trees lose their leaves .... winter.

6 I was born .... 13ᵗʰ August .... 1990.

7 I'll be in Madrid .... Christmas Eve.

8 They came back .... four o'clock .... the morning.

9 I often have to work .... night.

10 Life will be very different .... the 25ᵗʰ century.

11 I met him .... my birthday.

12 I'm sorry but Mr Newton is very busy .... the moment.

13 .... midday, the sun will be directly over our heads.

14 The First World War broke out .... August, 1914.

2 Complete with *by* or *until*.

Tip
With **by**, we refer to something that will **happen** by some time in the future.
With **until** we refer to something that will **last** until some time in the future.

1 I won't see her when she gets back. I will have left ....*by*........... then.

2 Let's go shopping. The shops are open .... half past two.

3 Kate's late. She should have been here .... now.

4 I can't come with you. I have to finish this article .... tomorrow.

5 No, I'm not leaving. I'll be here .... five.

6 We don't have much time. We have to be at the airport .... nine thirty.

7 David is in Spain. He'll be away .... Saturday.

8 Don't call him now. Wait .... tomorrow.

3 Complete with *during* or *while*.

1 I saw Tim ...while... I was waiting for the bus.

2 She was so tired that she fell asleep .... the meeting.

3 The phone rang .... I was in the shower.

4 I'll be studying for the History test .... the weekend.

5 Helen called .... you were sleeping.

6 You must not speak .... the exam.

7 I woke up twice .... the night.

8 This letter came .... you were out.

9 No one spoke .... the journey.

10 I found this old photograph .... I was cleaning my room.

B Prepositions of place

▶ Prepositions of place indicate a place. Some of these are:

at (at a point)	Mike is **at** the office.
on (on)	I left a note **on** the kitchen table.
over (over)	Let's hang the painting **over** the sofa.
above (above)	There's a sign **above** the entrance.
in (in)	My purse was **in** my bag five minutes ago!
inside (inside)	Let's see what's **inside** that box.
outside (outside)	He's been standing **outside** the bank for hours.
under (under)	There's a mouse **under** the sofa!
below (below)	I usually wear my skirts **below** the knee.
near (near)	Is there a bank **near** here?
next to (next to)	The cinema is **next to** the post office.
beside (beside)	They have a beautiful house **beside** the river.
by (by)	We sat **by** the fire to get warm.
in front of (in front of)	She parked her car **in front of** our house.
behind (behind)	The shop assistant was standing **behind** the counter.
opposite (opposite)	Let's put the bed **opposite** the window.
among (among many)	I found this magazine **among** some old books.
between (between two)	Liam is sitting **between** Jill and Tom.

▶ We use specific prepositions with some expressions.

at	on	in
at home	on the left/right	in bed
at school	on the first/second floor	in hospital
at work	on page 25	in prison
at the top/bottom (of)	on an island	in London/Greece
		in the middle (of)
		in the sky

▶ Please note the following:
- **in** Willow Street BUT **at** 25, Willow Street
- **on a chair** BUT **in** an armchair
- **on** a bus/train/plane/ship/bike/horse BUT **in** a car/taxi

C **Prepositions of movement**
Prepositions of movement indicate movement and are usually used with verbs that indicate movement, such as **come, go, walk, move, fly** etc.

up (up)	Let's go **up** that mountain.
down (down)	She ran **down** the stairs.
onto (onto)	The cat jumped **onto** the bed.
into (into)	He got **into** his car and left.
out of (out of)	Get **out of** my room now!
from (from)	I come home **from** work at six.
to (to)	Do you usually walk **to** school?
towards (towards)	I saw her walking **towards** me.
over (over)	The dog jumped **over** the wall.
round (round))	Go **round** the corner.
along (along)	Let's go for a walk **along** the river.
across (across, to the opposite side)	He swam **across** the river.
off (off, indicates going away)	The little boy fell **off** his bike.
past (by, with the meaning 'pass somebody/ something and leave him/ it behind')	I walked **past** Jane's house this morning.
through (between, through)	We drove **through** the tunnel.

Let's go up that mountain.

4 Circle the correct answer.

1 He hid the flowers *beside* / *behind* his back.
2 Olivia has been *in* / *at* hospital for two weeks now.
3 The manager's full name was printed *below* / *down* her signature.
4 We hung the painting *on* / *over* the fireplace.
5 I wasn't *in* / *at* home last night.
6 The boy standing *between* / *among* Grace and Maria is my cousin.
7 His office is *in* / *at* 25, Cherry Street.
8 Our flat is *on* / *in* the 5ᵗʰ floor.
9 Ms Sims sat *on* / *in* an armchair by the fire and told us a story.
10 You'll see the bus stop *in* / *on* your left.
11 The bank is *in* / *on* Wellington Street.
12 There is one black sheep *between* / *among* all the white sheep.
13 They stood *out* / *outside* the gate and waited.
14 Look at the list of words *on* / *in* page 316.

5 Circle the correct answer.

1 The Earth goes *towards* / *round* the Sun.
2 We took a long walk *along* / *through* the river.
3 A car hit him while he was walking *through* / *across* the road.
4 We stood up when the teacher walked *into* / *to* the classroom.
5 The burglars got in *across* / *through* the kitchen window.
6 I jumped *over* / *onto* the train while it was moving.
7 She walked *past* / *through* me without saying hello.
8 He fell *out of* / *off* the ladder and broke his leg.
9 Bob stood up and walked *towards* / *along* the door.
10 She walked out *of* / *off* the room with a strange look on her face.

D   Dependent prepositions

Verb dependent prepositions
Some verbs are followed by specific prepositions. Some of these are:

agree with	believe in	disagree about sth	listen to	talk about
apologise for	belong to	dream about	look at	tell sb about
apply for	borrow from	escape from	pay for	thank sb for
argue with sb	consist of	explain to	reply to	think about
argue about sth	crash into	hear from/about	search for	wait for
arrive in/at	depend on	laugh at	shout at	write to
ask for/about	disagree with sb	lie about	take care of	worry about

I wish you'd stop shouting at me!
She apologised for being late.

Adjective dependent prepositions
Some adjectives are followed by specific prepositions. Some of these are:

addicted to	dependent on	full of	nervous about	scared of
afraid of	different from	good at	proud of	similar to
angry with sb	dressed in	guilty of	ready for	sorry about/for
angry about sth	enthusiastic about	interested in	responsible for	sure of/about
bad at	excited about	jealous of	sad about	surprised at/by
bored with	fed up with	keen on	(the) same as	tired of
connected to	fond of	made of	satisfied with	worried about
crazy about				

I'm not very good at Maths.
Mark is crazy about football.
I've always been interested in History.

Nouns and prepositions
Some nouns are followed by specific prepositions. Some of these are:

advice on/about	description of	interest in	reason for
answer to	difficulty in/with	invitation to	responsibility for
cause of	discussion on/about	lack of	result of
cost of	example of	need for	solution to
demand for	information about/on	photo/picture of	

She gave them a detailed description of the robbers.
They have not found a solution to the problem yet.

---

6   Complete with a *preposition*.

1   I agree ……with…… Diane.

2   You should thank him ………………… his help.

3   Don't worry ………………… me. I'm fine.

4   Tina is in Italy, so I'm taking care ………………… her cat for a few days.

5   Do you believe ………………… miracles?

6   How much did you pay ………………… those sunglasses?

7   You can always depend ………………… me.

8   We borrowed £400 ………………… Stephen.

9   He apologised ………………… being late.

10   Does this book belong ………………… you?

11   The team consists ………………… six players.

12   What are you two talking …………………?

13   Gemma is waiting ………………… us at the station.

14   I'm afraid I disagree ………………… you.

15   He lost control of the car and crashed ………………… a tree.

16   Have you thought ………………… their offer?

17   The police are searching ………………… the missing child.

18   What time does the plane arrive ………………… London?

7 Complete with a *preposition*.

1 Bruce is not very keen ....*on*.......... sport.

2 I'm really sorry .... what I said last night.

3 Well done! I'm so proud .... you!

4 Are you still angry .... him?

5 She's really excited .... moving to London.

6 That car is similar .... ours.

7 He hasn't called yet and I'm very worried .... him.

8 I'm fed up .... your lies!

9 She's afraid .... heights.

10 Who's responsible .... all this mess?

8 Complete with a *preposition*.

1 The cost ....*of*.......... that house was too high for us.

2 This is a photo .... Alex and me in Paris.

3 Who can give me an example .... an irregular verb?

4 What are his reasons .... leaving the country?

5 They've been trying to find a solution .... this problem for years.

6 I couldn't find the answer .... his question.

7 We soon lost interest .... the game.

8 I would like some more information .... this product.

9 What was the cause .... the fire?

10 She has sent us an invitation .... her birthday party.

9 Read and complete. Use only one word in each space.

I remember waking up (1) ....*at*.......... five that morning. I got (2) .... of bed as fast as I could and started getting ready (3) .... the big day. I had been waiting (4) .... this day for weeks. I had always been interested (5) .... fashion and I really wanted the job.

I left the house (6) .... eight and arrived (7) .... the office ten minutes before the interview. Finally, a secretary told me that Mr Jones, the manager, would like to see me. I took a deep breath and walked (8) .... his office.

I felt really nervous (9) .... the interview. Mr Jones asked me (10) .... my previous experience, my studies and my interests. He listened (11) .... me very carefully and gave me some more information (12) .... the job.

When I had answered all his questions, he stood up and said: 'Thank you (13) .... your time, Ms Brown. I think you're perfect for this job. Can you start work (14) .... Monday?'

I could not believe my ears! I accepted his offer, of course. I smiled, thanked him and walked out (15) .... his office. I had finally found the job of my dreams!

Oral practice Now you can do the **oral activity** for **Unit 18** (Teacher's Resource File).

Phrasal verbs

I know the cost of living is **going up** all the time. But don't you think we should **look for** other ways to cut costs?

Grammar reference

See **Phrasal verbs, pages 153-155.**

A   Phrasal verbs

Phrasal verbs are verbs that usually consist of two words. One word is always a verb and the second may be a preposition or an adverb **(particle)**.
I'm looking for my keys.
Our car broke down on the way home.

Intransitive phrasal verbs

Some **phrasal verbs** are intransitive, ie. they do not take an object. They usually consist of a verb and an adjective or an adverb **(particle)**.
I grew up in London.
Look out! We're going to crash!

Transitive phrasal verbs
Some **phrasal verbs** are transitive, ie. they take an object.

▶ When the object is a noun, it can go:
• between the verb and the **particle.**
  She turned the light on.
• after the **particle.**
  She turned on the light.

▶ When the object of the clause is a pronoun, not a noun, then this goes between the verb and the **particle.** It cannot go after the particle.
  She turned it on.
  ~~**She turned on it.**~~ ✗

▶ There are some **phrasal verbs** which, even if they do take an object, can never be separated. That is, the object cannot go between the two parts of the **phrasal verb,** but always goes after the particle. Some of these are: **look after, deal with, get over, take after.**
  Maria takes after her mother.
  ~~**Maria takes her mother after.**~~ ✗

B Phrasal verbs with three parts

There are some phrasal verbs that consist of three parts: the verb, the particle and a preposition, eg. **come up with, look forward to.** The object of these verbs goes at the end of the sentence, not between the parts of the **phrasal verb.**
We look forward to hearing from you.

Grammar practice

I Match and write sentences. Then write T if the phrasal verb is transitive or I if it is intransitive.

1	A fire broke	a	you off at the post office.
2	We haven't heard	b	up early yesterday.
3	I got	c	after her mother.
4	We are looking	d	out during the night.
5	I'll drop	e	off in the middle of the night.
6	The alarm went	f	from Andrew lately.
7	My father grew	g	up in Scotland.
8	Sarah takes	h	forward to our holiday.

Tip
Transitive phrasal verbs
are those that take an object.
Intransitive phrasal verbs are those that do not take an object.

1 A fire broke out during the night. ....I....
2 ....
3 ....
4 ....
5 ....
6 ....
7 ....
8 ....

145

2 Rewrite the sentences replacing the underlined words with a pronoun.

> **Tip**
>
> Remember that when the object of the **phrasal verb** is a pronoun, then this can only go between the two parts of the verb, not after the **particle**.

1 Take off <u>that silly hat</u>.
Take it off.

2 We really should throw away <u>this old chair</u>.
....

3 Will you please turn down <u>the music</u>?
....

4 Put on <u>your coat</u>.
....

5 I'd like to try on <u>those shoes</u>.
....

6 The teacher gave out <u>the tests</u>.
....

7 I turned on <u>the radio</u> to listen to the news.
....

3 Complete with the correct *particle*.

break

1 The car broke ......*down*...... in the middle of our trip.

2 Mike and Sue were together for five years. They broke .... last month.

3 World War II broke .... in 1939.

4 Have they found the man who broke .... your office last week?

5 The prisoners broke .... of jail last night.

4 Circle the correct answer.

bring

1 She was born in France but she was brought ..... in Morocco.
a round   b about
c along   (d) up

2 Don't forget to bring your sister ..... next time you come to visit.
a about   b along
c up   d on

3 She was unconscious after the accident but we managed to bring her ..... .
a along   b round
c back   d up

4 I don't think this is important but let's talk about it since you brought it ..... .
a round   b up
c back   d about

5 Tom was brought ..... by his aunt after his parents died.
a back   b about
c along   d up

6 Has Maria brought ..... the book she borrowed last week?
a back   b about
c round   d up

5 Complete with the correct *particle(s)*.

come

1 I came ......*across*...... this old book while I was tidying my room.

2 It took him two hours to come .... after the operation.

3 He's been in bed for three days. He's come .... the flu.

4 You're going to the cinema, aren't you? Can I come .... too?

5 I'm afraid I can't join you. Something important has come ....

6 When is your sister coming .... from Spain?

7 We didn't know what to do. Then Danny came .... a brilliant idea.

6 Circle the correct answer.

get

1 I got *off* / *down* the bus and walked home.

2 Those children are always getting *up to* / *along* something.

3 The police arrested one of the thieves. The other one got *off* / *away*.

4 She doesn't get *away* / *on* with her boss, so she's looking for a new job.

5 After waiting for almost an hour, I finally got *on* / *up* the train at nine.

6 Although he didn't like her when they first met, they get *along* / *across* fine now.

7 The doctor said that it would take her more than a week to get *off* / *over* her illness.

8 Stop watching TV and get *along* / *down to* work!

7 Complete with a *phrasal verb* with *go*.

go

1 No, you don't understand. Let's ......*go over*...... this again.

2 Suddenly, all the lights .... and I couldn't see anything.

3 The policeman .... the thief but didn't manage to catch him.

4 Don't drink that milk. It has ....

5 I asked her to be quiet but she .... talking.

6 I was late for work this morning. My alarm clock didn't ....

7 Things are getting more and more expensive every day. Prices .... all the time.

8 Complete with the correct *particle(s)*.

keep

1 You'll have to keep ......*off*...... the grass.

2 Slow down! I can't keep .... you!

3 There was a sign that said 'Keep ....', so we didn't go inside the room.

4 The police warned us to keep .... the building because it wasn't safe.

5 Don't give up. Keep .... trying.

9 Circle the correct answer.

look

1 Look *after* / *out*! Someone's behind us!

2 I look *forward to* / *up to* seeing you again next week.

3 The police are going to look *in* / *into* the cause of the fire.

4 Don't worry. I'll look *out* / *after* the baby while you're out.

5 If you don't know the meaning of this word, look it *up* / *for* in the dictionary.

6 She looks *up to* / *down on* us. She thinks she's better than we are.

7 I've been looking *for* / *after* my keys for hours. Have you seen them?

8 Everyone admires and looks *up* / *up to* her.

10 Complete with the correct *particle(s)*.

make

1 Is this story true or did you make it all ....*up*........?

2 The burglars made .... £1,000.

3 They had a fight but they made .... a few minutes later.

4 You could have made .... a better excuse!

5 Her handwriting is terrible. I can't make it .... at all.

11 Circle the correct answer.

put

1 Put the knife *up* / (*back*) when you've finished with it.

2 – I'd like to speak to the manager.
– Just a moment. I'll put you *down* / *through*.

3 I couldn't find a room, so Bob *put me up* / *put me off* for the night.

4 The meeting will be put *away* / *off* until next month.

5 I can't read this. I'll have to put *on* / *away* my glasses.

6 The fire spread quickly. It took them two hours to *put it off* / *put it out*.

7 The horse had broken its leg, so they had to *put it up* / *put it down*.

8 I don't know why she puts *up with* / *up* his behaviour!

12 Complete with the correct *particle(s)*.

run

1 I ran ......*into*...... Mike this morning.

2 We've run .... coffee. Please go to the supermarket and get some.

3 He ran .... from home when he was sixteen and has lived alone ever since.

4 Her dog was run .... by a car yesterday.

5 Sue left and James ran .... her to tell her he was sorry.

6 I ran .... an old friend in town the other day.

13 Complete with the correct *particle*.

take

1 It was hot, so I took ....*off*.......... my coat.

2 I'm really sorry. I take .... what I said last night.

3 She takes .... her father. They have the same looks and personality.

4 She went to the dentist and had a tooth taken ....

5 Our plane took .... at 9.00 and we arrived in London at 12.30.

6 He took .... tennis six months ago.

14 Circle the correct answer.

turn

1 The princess kissed the frog and it turned (*into*) / *in* a prince.

2 I didn't know what to do so I turned *into* / *to* him for help.

3 It's dark in here. Could you turn *on* / *off* the light?

4 It's hot in here. Let's turn *up* / *down* the heating.

5 We invited fifteen people but only ten turned *on* / *up*.

6 Turn the TV *up* / *off*. No one's watching it.

7 They offered him a job but he turned it *up* / *down*.

15 Complete with the correct *particle*.

miscellaneous

1 I'm late. Can you drop me ......*off*...... at the station?

2 I have to go. We'll carry .... our discussion later.

3 I got up at six and set .... for London at half past seven.

4 They didn't want those old clothes, so they gave them ....

5 I can't hear you. Can you speak .... please?

6 I had to be at the airport at five, so I checked .... of the hotel at three.

7 This suit would look great on you. Why don't you try it ....?

8 Could you lend me £15? I'll pay you .... tomorrow.

9 He had to give .... football when he broke his leg.

10 The building wasn't safe after the earthquake, so they pulled it ....

11 The game was called .... because of the rain.

12 Mum told me .... for being late.

13 The house was rather old, so we had to do it .... before moving in.

14 You're acting like a four-year-old! Will you ever grow ....?

15 I'm not sure if I'll accept their offer. I need more time to think it ....

16 Don't worry. You can count .... me.

17 Can you hold .... a minute while I get my bag?

18 I'm sorry I'm late. I dropped .... to see Jane on my way home.

16 Read and complete. Use only one word in each space.

·· Saving Grace ··········

I had never thought of getting a pet until Grace, an adorable little puppy, turned (1) .... on our doorstep two years ago. She was so tired and hungry that we decided to look (2) .... her for the night and take her to the animal shelter in the morning. I wanted to keep her, but my mother didn't want a dog in the house.

When we took Grace to the animal shelter, a vet examined her and told us that she had a serious disease. He said there was no hope for her and he would have to put her (3) ....

'But there must be something we can do,' I thought. I begged my mother to let me keep Grace. Mum didn't like my idea at first but she gave (4) ....

We took her home and did everything we could for her. We turned (5) .... several other vets for help. One of them told us he could help her. And he did. Grace got (6) .... her illness three months later.

She is now three years old and she's never been healthier in her life. In fact, she gave birth to three puppies last week. They all take (7) .... her. They're as clever and adorable as she is. Mum loves them too. Well, who knows? Perhaps I can talk Mum (8) .... keeping them!

Maureen Brown, 15

Oral practice Now you can do the **oral activity** for **Unit 19** (Teacher's Resource File).

Revision 14-19

1 Rewrite the sentences using the word given.

0 Myra said to me, 'We're getting married next week.' **following**
   Myra told me that they _were getting married the following_ week.

1 'Have you told Lisa about the party?' I asked him. **if**
   I asked him .... Lisa about the party.

2 Ivan said to me, 'I saw her yesterday.' **had**
   Ivan told me that he .... day.

3 'Please leave me alone!' she told him. **to**
   She asked .... alone.

4 'How much did your CD player cost?' he asked me. **wanted**
   He .... my CD player had cost.

5 'I must stay until Ross comes back,' she said. **to**
   She said that .... until Ross came back.

10

2 Read and circle the correct answer.

Two weeks ago, our class visited Kensington Palace, (0) ..c.. is one of the most famous buildings in London. The palace, (1) ..... has been the home of many of Britain's kings and queens, was built at the beginning of the seventeenth century. (2) ....., it did not become a palace until 1689, (3) ..... King William III bought it from the Earl of Nottingham.

The parts of the building (4) ..... are used by members of the Royal family are not open to the public, (5) ..... we didn't see the whole palace. (6) ....., we were able to see the room (7) ..... Queen Victoria slept. (8) ..... we only saw part of the palace, the guide had (9) ..... many things to tell us that the tour lasted for almost two hours. We all enjoyed our visit (10) ..... found everything very interesting.

0 a who	b whom	(c) which	d where
1 a who	b which	c where	d when
2 a Although	b However	c Whereas	d Despite
3 a which	b whom	c where	d when
4 a that	b where	c whom	d when
5 a so that	b so	c because of	d because
6 a In spite of	b Despite	c But	d However
7 a which	b in that	c in where	d where
8 a Although	b Despite	c In spite of	d But
9 a such	b such a	c so	d so that
10 a while	b whereas	c but	d and

10

3 Rewrite the sentences using the word given.

0 'Yes, I cheated in the exam,' the boy said. **that**
   The boy admitted _that he had cheated_ in the exam.

1 'He stole the jewellery!' she said. **accused**
   She .... the jewellery.

2 'No, I won't lend you my car,' my brother told me. **refused**
   My brother .... his car.

3 'Don't stay in the sun for more than an hour,' she told me. **advised**
   She .... in the sun for more than an hour.

4 'I'll be back before dinner,' he said. **promised**
   He .... back before dinner.

5 'I'm sorry I was so rude,' she said. **apologised**
   She .... so rude.

4 Complete with a *preposition*.

0 I didn't know you were scared ......_of_...... dogs.
1 Stop worrying .... the exam. I'm sure you'll do just fine.
2 There's a solution .... every problem.
3 Our office is .... 53, West Street.
4 Have you always been interested .... art?
5 I had to borrow some money .... my parents.
6 We're leaving for Canada .... 5th March.
7 They're really proud .... their daughter.
8 He had a bad accident last week. He's .... hospital.
9 The Head Teacher's office is .... the second floor.
10 That building is a typical example .... modern architecture.

5 Complete with the correct *particle*.

0 Look ......_out_......! You're going to fall!
1 I don't feel very well. I think I'm coming .... with a cold.
2 Was that a true story or did you make it ....?
3 How's Tom? I haven't heard .... him for ages.
4 Stephen lent me £500 last month. I haven't paid him .... yet.
5 I don't know what this word means. I'll have to look it .... in a dictionary.
6 He was born in Wales but he grew .... in London.
7 It's cold. Why don't you put .... your coat?
8 We look forward .... seeing you again on Friday.
9 They were walking too fast and I couldn't keep up .... them.
10 My car has broken .... again, so I have to take it to the garage.

Spelling rules

Present simple

In the present simple, in the third person singular:

▶ In verbs that end in **–ss, –ch, –sh, –x** and **–o,** we add the ending **–es.**
kiss – kisses **touch – touches** **mix – mixes**
▶ When a verb ends in **–y** and before this there is a consonant, the **–y** comes off and we add the ending **–ies.**
tidy – tidies **study – studies** **cry – cries**
▶ But when there is a vowel before the **–y,** as a rule, we add **–s.**
buy – buys **play – plays** **enjoy – enjoys**

Present participle

To form the present participle, we add the ending **–ing.** The spelling of some verbs changes, ie.:

▶ Verbs that end in **–e** drop the **–e** before the **–ing** ending.
come – coming **make – making**
▶ Monosyllabic verbs that end in a consonant and where before this, there is just one vowel, double the final consonant before the **–ing** ending.
run – running (and **eat – eating**)
▶ Verbs with two or more syllables that end in a consonant, and where there is a vowel that is stressed before this, double the final consonant before the **–ing** ending.
begin – beginning (There is a vowel and it is stressed. The final consonant is doubled.)
open – opening (There is a vowel but it is not stressed. The final consonant is not doubled.)
▶ Verbs that end in **–l** double the **–l** before the **–ing** ending.
travel – travelling

Past simple

For the past simple of regular verbs:

▶ In verbs that end in **–e,** we only add **–d.**
dance – danced **live – lived**
▶ When a verb ends in **–y,** and where before this there is a consonant, the **–y** comes off and we add **–ied.**
cry – cried **study – studied**
▶ When a verb ends in **–y** and before this there is a vowel, as a rule, we add **–ed**
play – played **enjoy – enjoyed**
▶ Monosyllabic verbs that end in a consonant and where before this there is just one vowel, the final consonant is doubled before the **–ed** ending.
plan – planned **stop – stopped**
▶ However, this does not apply to monosyllabic verbs that end in **–w, –x,** or **–z.**
fix – fixed **mix – mixed**
▶ Verbs that end in **–l** double the final **–l** before the **–ed** ending.
travel – travelled

Comparison of adjectives

With regard to the comparative and superlative form of adjectives:

▶ When an adjective ends in **–e,** then in the comparative form, we just add **–r** while in the superlative form, just **–st.**
large – larger – largest   nice – nicer – nicest

▶ Monosyllabic adjectives that end in a consonant, and where before this there is a vowel, double the final consonant in the comparative and superlative form..
hot – hotter – hottest   fat – fatter – fattest

▶ When an adjective ends in **–y,** then the –y comes off and we add the ending **–ier** for the comparative and the ending **–iest** for the superlative.
heavy – heavier – heaviest   easy – easier – easiest

Adverbs

To form adverbs

▶ When an adjective ends in **–y,** then the –y comes off and we add the ending **–ily** to the end of the adjective.
heavy – heavily   easy – easily

▶ In adjectives that end in **–l,** as a rule, we add **–ly.**
careful – carefully (carefuly)   **wonderful – wonderfully** (wonderfuly)

Phrasal verbs

break down = break down (equipment, cars, etc.)

break out = (1) break out (fires, war, etc.) (2) escape

break up = break up, cease a relationship/marriage

bring about = cause, bring about

bring sb/sth along = bring somebody or something with me

bring back = return something (to somebody)

bring on = cause

call off = call off, cancel

carry on = carry on, continue to do something

check in = register/sign during my arrival at a hotel

check out = leave a hotel, returning the key and paying my bill

clean up = clean up, tidy

come across = meet/find by chance

come along = (1) follow, go with somebody (2) progress, come along

come back (from) = come back, return

come down with sth = 'catch' an illness

come round = (1) recover, regain my senses (2) visit, drop in on somebody

come up with = mention, come up (a subject)

come up with = find, think of (an idea, a solution, etc.)

count on = count on somebody

do up = repair, renovate

drop by = visit somebody or go somewhere (usually for a little while and without having planned it) drop off = take (something/somebody) somewhere in a car

fill in = fill in (eg. a form)

get (sth) across (to sb) = explain/make something clear to somebody

get along (with sb) = get on well with somebody

get away = get away, escape

get away with sth = avoid something bad or unpleasant, 'get away with it'

get down to = to work seriously/deal (with something)

get off = disembark, get off (a bus, train, etc.)

get on = embark, get on (a bus, train, etc.)

get on (with sb) = get on well (with somebody)

get over = get over (an illness, a fear, etc.)

get round to sth = manage to do something that I have wanted to do for a long time

get up = wake up, get up

get up to sth = 'get up to', do something bad

give away = (1) give away (2) disclose (something secret)

give in = submit, give in

give out = share, distribute   give up = stop a habit

go ahead = proceed with something, do something that I planned to do

go down with = 'catch' an illness

go off = go off (food)

go off = start to make a noise (alarms, alarm clocks, etc.)

go on = carry on, continue to do something

go out = go out (fire or light)

go over = explain (something to somebody)

go up = increase (price/cost)

grow out of sth = stop doing something/being interested in something as I grow up

grow up = grow up, mature

hand in = hand in something (eg. a project)

hear from = have/find out news (from somebody)

hold back = keep something secret

hold on = wait/hold on (usually when we ask somebody to wait)

keep (sb) away from = keep or hold somebody away from something

keep off = keep away from, avoid (eg. food)

keep on = carry on, continue to do something

keep (sb) out = keep or hold somebody out (of a building)

keep up with = keep up (with somebody or something)

let sb down = disappoint (somebody)

look after = look after, take care of

look down on = look down on, consider oneself superior to somebody else

look for = look for, search

look into = examine, investigate (a crime, a problem, etc.)

look up = look for information (in a book, a list, etc.)

look up to = admire (somebody)

make off with sth = steal/grab something and leave

make out = see/hear/realise (something) with difficulty

make up = think of, make up, find (an excuse, a story, etc.)

make up = get back together with somebody after an argument

make sth up to sb = compensate somebody for something, pay somebody back for a favour

pay back = (1) pay off (a debt)
                  (2) take revenge

pick on = behave badly to somebody, pick on

pick up = go and get (somebody from somewhere)

pull down = demolish (a building intentionally)

put away = put something in its place, where it usually is

put back = return something to its place

put down = kill, commit euthanasia (animals)

put on = put on (clothes)

put out = extinguish (a fire, a cigarette, etc.)

put through = connect (by telephone)

put up = put up (somebody)

run across = meet somebody or find by chance

run after = chase (somebody or something)

run away = run away, escape

run into = meet somebody by chance/unexpectedly

run out of = run out of, have no more of something

run over = hit (somebody or something) with a car

set off = start a journey

show off = show off (knowledge, abilities, wealth, etc.)

shut down = stop working (eg. a machine)

speak up = increase the pitch of my voice

stand out = be distinguished, be obvious

stay up = stay up, stay awake

take after = look like, take somebody's features

take back = revoke, 'take back' something that I said

take off = take off (a piece of clothing)

take out = take out, remove

take over = take over, take control

take up = start (a sport, a hobby, etc.)

talk sb into sth = convince somebody to do something

talk sb out of sth = convince somebody not to do sth

tell off = scold, tell somebody off

think over/through = reconsider, think about something more carefully

try on = try on (a piece of clothing)

turn down = reduce (the volume, the sound, etc.)

turn into = change into, become

turn off = turn off (the light, equipment, etc.)

turn on = turn on (the light, equipment, etc.)

turn to = turn to somebody (for help, advice, etc.)

turn up = arrive, appear somewhere

turn up = increase, turn up (the volume, the sound, etc.)

All tenses reference chart

Tenses of the Active Voice

Tense	Regular verb	Irregular verb
Present simple	I call	I choose
Present continuous	I am calling	I am choosing
Present perfect simple	I have called	I have chosen
Present perfect continuous	I have been calling	I have been choosing
Past simple	I called	I chose
Past continuous	I was calling	I was choosing
Past perfect simple	I had called	I had chosen
Past perfect continuous	I had been calling	I had been choosing
will	I will call	I will choose
going to	I am going to call	I am going to choose
Future continuous	I will be calling	I will be choosing
Future perfect simple	I will have called	I will have chosen
Future perfect continuous	I will have been calling	I will have been choosing
Infinitive	to call	to choose
Perfect infinitive	to have called	to have chosen
Gerund	calling	choosing
Perfect gerund	having called	having chosen

Tenses of the Passive Voice

Tense	Regular verb	Irregular verb
Present simple	I am called	I am chosen
Present continuous	I am being called	I am being chosen
Present perfect simple	I have been called	I have been chosen
Past simple	I was called	I was chosen
Past continuous	I was being called	I was being chosen
Past perfect simple	I had been called	I had been chosen
will	I will be called	I will be chosen
going to	I am going to be called	I am going to be chosen
Future perfect simple	I will have been called	I will have been chosen
Infinitive	to be called	to be chosen
Perfect infinitive	to have been called	to have been chosen
Gerund	being called	being chosen
Perfect gerund	having been called	having been chosen

Irregular verbs

Infinitive	Past	Past participle	Infinitive	Past	Past participle
be	was/were	been	light	lit	lit
beat	beat	beaten	lose	lost	lost
become	became	become	make	made	made
begin	began	begun	mean	meant	meant
bend	bent	bent	meet	met	met
bet	bet	bet	pay	paid	paid
bind	bound	bound	put	put	put
bite	bit	bitten	read	read	read
blow	blew	blown	ride	rode	ridden
break	broke	broken	ring	rang	rung
bring	brought	brought	rise	rose	risen
broadcast	broadcast	broadcast	run	ran	run
build	built	built	say	said	said
burst	burst	burst	see	saw	seen
buy	bought	bought	seek	sought	sought
cast	cast	cast	sell	sold	sold
catch	caught	caught	send	sent	sent
choose	chose	chosen	set	set	set
come	came	come	sew	sewed	sewn
cost	cost	cost	shake	shook	shaken
creep	crept	crept	shine	shone	shone
cut	cut	cut	shoot	shot	shot
deal	dealt	dealt	show	showed	shown/showed
dig	dug	dug	shrink	shrank	shrunk
do	did	done	shut	shut	shut
draw	drew	drawn	sing	sang	sung
drink	drank	drunk	sink	sank	sunk
drive	drove	driven	sit	sat	sat
eat	ate	eaten	sleep	slept	slept
fall	fell	fallen	slide	slid	slid
feed	fed	fed	sow	sowed	sown
feel	felt	felt	speak	spoke	spoken
fight	fought	fought	spend	spent	spent
find	found	found	spit	spat	spat
flee	fled	fled	split	split	split
fly	flew	flown	spread	spread	spread
forbid	forbade	forbidden	spring	sprang	sprung
forget	forgot	forgotten	stand	stood	stood
forgive	forgave	forgiven	steal	stole	stolen
freeze	froze	frozen	stick	stuck	stuck
get	got	got	sting	stung	stung
give	gave	given	stink	stank	stunk
go	went	gone	strike	struck	struck
grow	grew	grown	swear	swore	sworn
hang	hung	hung	sweep	swept	swept
have	had	had	swim	swam	swum
hear	heard	heard	swing	swung	swung
hide	hid	hidden	take	took	taken
hit	hit	hit	teach	taught	taught
hold	held	held	tear	tore	torn
hurt	hurt	hurt	tell	told	told
keep	kept	kept	think	thought	thought
kneel	knelt	knelt	throw	threw	thrown
know	knew	known	understand	understood	understood
lay	laid	laid	wake	woke	woken
lead	led	led	wear	wore	worn
leave	left	left	weep	wept	wept
lend	lent	lent	win	won	won
let	let	let	write	wrote	written
lie	lay	lain			

Wordlist

Unit 1
issue
absolutely
prepare
feature
immediately
notice
include
contain
forehead
have a temperature
upset
concentrate
take place
event
take part
mud
dig
attic

Unit 2
burglar
spinach
lose interest
excursion
pull down = (intentionally)
demolish a building
hook
monolingual = who knows or
uses just one language
(be) out of breath = be
breathless, be out of breath
graduate
intruder
realise
(be) out of breath
exhausted
garlic
sore = sore (e.g. from the sun)
adventure
reunite
wander
explore
distance

Unit 3
bet
expect
suppose
certainly = certainly,
undoubtedly
weather forecast
accept
branch
leak
pick up = go and get
somebody from somewhere
exhibition
chemist
well-known = well-known,
famous
award
autobiography
medicine
mess
solar

eclipse
task
perform = perform, carry out
operation = (surgical)
operation
manufacturer
double = become double,
double

Unit 4
speech = speech, talk
Thai
suggest
What's the rush? = Why are
you hurrying? There is no
reason to hurry.
plenty

Revision 1–4
take time off (work) = take
leave
deserve = deserve, I deserve
look for
crossing
solar-powered = that works
using solar power
come true

Unit 5
fair = (industrial) exhibition
owner
robotic
incredible = incredible,
fantastic
local
escape
clue = clue, indication
equipment
shop assistant = salesperson
(in a shop)
make the bed
switch on = switch on (the
light, equipment, etc.)
pour = serve (a drink)
slice
balcony
licence

Unit 6
tip
comfortable
area = area, place
take a break
panic
weekday = weekday, working
day
cancel
button
give sb a lift = go with
somebody somewhere in a
car
queue = wait in the queue
affect
caffeine
rude
nearly

keep fit = keep in good
physical condition
definitely
increase
circulation
sweat

Unit 7
careless
save up = save (money)
instructions
fail
offer
wing
lend
tricky = complex, complicated
admit
ruin
put on = put on (clothes)
elder = older (in age)
nightmare
refuse
advice
directions
critic
review = review (of a book,
film, etc.)
get on with sb
look after = look after, take
care of
disappointed
give sb a ring
change my mind
lottery ticket = lottery ticket,
draw ticket
unemployed
stay up = stay up, stay
awake

Unit 8
only child
lonely = alone, lonely
afford = have enough money
for something
bossy
clean up = tidy up, clean
chance
broke = penniless, broke
pity
pay back = pay off (a debt)

Revision 5–8
box office
play
shrink = 'contract', 'shrink' (in
size)

Unit 9
fluffy
Stone Age
preserve
sand
dust
blow off = blow sth off
obey
space probe = space probe

contact
deliver
hold = conduct (e.g. a
meeting)
species = species (e.g. animal)
vet
examine
treat
assist
prime minister
announcement
restore = restore, reconstruct
question
sting = prick, sting (with
regard to an insect)
pick = gather (e.g. flowers)
exhibit
bride
salary
brochure
pay rise = increase (in salary)
estimate
report
genius
endangered = at risk of
becoming extinct
critically = dangerously,
critically
threaten
illegally
strict
introduce
environmental
colleague
injure
parcel = parcel, packet
creature = being, creature
exist
human being = person, human
being
effort
according to
extinct = that has
disappeared (e.g. animals)

Unit 10
tap
develop = develop
(photographs, film)
translate
rebuild = rebuild, reconstruct
install
tuner = the person whose
profession is to tune musical
instruments
tune
vacuum = clean (using an
electric brush)
dye
blood pressure
travel agent
arrangement
watchmaker
mansion = mansion, villa
fabulous = fabulous, excellent
plant
invitation

Unit 11

successful
form
adapt
soil
commonly = commonly, usually
pollen
reproduce
raise = amass, gather
occasionally
necklace
scarf
cardboard
patiently
reptile
swallow
wide = wide, broad
cyanide
substance
sensitive
weigh
safe
greedy
novel
patient
complicated
focus = focus, concentrate my interest on something
eyesight
hawk
sharp
beat
flexible
skeleton

Unit 12

seem = seem, give the impression
arrange
beg
force
manage
pretend
remind
regret
anxious
willing
furious
behave
vote
in public
impatient
beat
freeze
audience = public, audience
avoid
deny
look forward to
mention
quit = stop, quit
recommend = suggest, recommend
can't help = cannot do (something)
feel like = be in the mood for
accuse

first class = first class (e.g. on an aeroplane)
neighbourhood
share
lifestyle
choice
Thank goodness = Thank goodness, Thank God
intend
cheer = cheer, shout hurray
iron
mop
swap
thoughtful = polite, somebody who considers others
expression
unwrap

Unit 13

fold
herring
iceberg
heat
cotton
anger
democracy
baggage = luggage, baggage
behaviour
luggage = luggage, baggage
research
carton
gram
sachet
tube
binoculars
tights
goods
crew
staff
economics = economics, economic (science)
measles
mumps = parotitis, mumps
means
series
persuade
margarine
drawer
parliament = parliament, House of Commons
homeless
originate
slave
native = native, indigenous
issue
postage stamp = (postage) stamp
definition
product
silence
baron
dandy = excellent, fabulous
pedal
propel = propel, instigate
blacksmith
wheel
safety

Revision 9–13

reception
formula = recipe, (mathematical or chemical) formula

Unit 14

competition
owe
security
enter = enter, go into
pay attention = pay attention, be careful
draw
abroad
cheque
judge
wonder
add
simulation
challenging
collection
special effects
edition
turn down = turn down (the volume, the sound, etc.)
shoot = shoot (a film)
unique
be based on
script

Unit 15

demand
forbid
warn
inform
selfish
edge = edge (e.g. of a cliff)
cliff
responsibility
responsible
cause
cheat = copy/'steal' in exams, cheat

Unit 16

birthplace
childhood
landmark
playwright = play writer
originally
fire brigade = fire (service)
proudly
annoying
talented
comedian
appearance
composer
countless
silent = silent, mute

Unit 17

lawn
perfectly
logical
lawyer
identify

melt
rent
book = make a reservation
contract
turn off = turn off (the light, equipment, etc.)
absent
succeed
muscle
pump
lung
absorb
shut down = stop (e.g. a machine) working
process
require
tiredness
objection
promote
guilty
hang-gliding
parachute
flow
surface
slope = (downhill) surface/slope
condition
reserve
get over = get over (e.g. an illness)

Unit 18

signature
fireplace
apply = apply, make an application
depend
consist
addicted
dependent
similar
demand
description
lack

Unit 19

cut costs = reduce/limit expenses
unconscious = unconscious, senseless
flu
illness
excuse
handwriting
spread
personality
adorable
shelter
disease

Revision 14–19

architecture

Pearson Education Limited
Edinburgh Gate
Harlow
Essex CM20 2JE
England
and Associated Companies throughout the World

www.longman.com
© Pearson Education Limited 2003
First published in 2003

The right of Maria Carling to be identified as the author of this Work
has been asserted by her in accordance with the Copyright,
Designs and Patents Act 1988.

ISBN-13: 978-0-582-77599-2
ISBN-10: 0-582-77599-x

Set in Gill Sans
Printed in Spain by Mateu Cromo
Third impression 2006

Acknowledgements

Author acknowledgements
The author would like to thank Tasia Vassilatou and Loukas Ioannou for
their invaluable contribution and support. Thanks also to Ms Vasiliki Drougouti
for her help and Georgia Zographou for always being there.

Publisher acknowledgements
The publishers would like to thank Ms Agapi Dendaki for her valuable help
in preparing this book.

Designed by Studio Image and Photographic Art
Illustrated by Peter Standley